E

MW00653851

The mythology of Indian plants

By Maneka Gandhi
1000 ANIMAL QUIZ

BRAHMA'S HAIR

The mythology of Indian plants

MANEKA GANDHI

With Yasmin Singh

Rupa & Co

Copyright © Maneka Gandhi 1989

First Published 1989
Seventh Impression 2007

Published by
Rupa & Co
7/16, Ansari Road, Daryaganj,
New Delhi 110 002

Sales Centres:

Allahabad Bangalore Chandigarh Chennai
Hyderabad Jaipur Kathmandu
Kolkata Mumbai Pune

Illustrations and Cover: Mona Bhandari

Typeset by
Megatechnics
19A Ansari Road
New Delhi 110 002

Printed in India by
Gopsons Papers Ltd.
A-14 Sector 60
Noida 201 301

CONTENTS

It is said that all plants are created from the hair of Brahma, the creator.

1

CORAL JASMINE TREE

Latin Name	*Nyctanthes arbor tristis*
English Names	*Queen of the Night, Coral Jasmine*
Indian Names	*Bengali : Shephalika, Siuli*
	Hindi : Harashringara
	Marathi : Parijata, Kharsati
	Sanskrit : Parijata
	Tamil : Parijata, Paghala
Family	Oleaceae

Nyctanthes means Night Flower and *arbor tristis* the Sad Tree. Parijata, the Sanskrit name, means descended from the sea. Harashringara is ornament of the gods or beautiful ornament.

The flowers are gathered for religious offerings and to make garlands. The orange heart is used for dyeing silk and cotton, a practice that started with Buddhist monks whose orange robes were given their colour by this flower.

The Parijata is regarded in Hindu mythology as one of the five wish-granting trees of Devaloka.

Why the Parijata blooms at night

A legend in the Vishnu Purana tells of a king who had a beautiful and sensitive daughter called Parijata. She fell in love with Surya, the sun. Leave your kingdom and be mine, said the sun passionately. Obediently Parijata shed her royal robes and followed her beloved.

But the sun grew cold as he was tired of Parijata and soon he deserted her and fled back to the sky.

The young princess died heartbroken. She was burnt on the funeral pyre and from her ashes grew a single tree. From its drooping branches grew the most beautiful flowers with deep orange hearts. But, since the flowers cannot bear the sight of the sun, they only bloom when it disappears from the sky and, as its first rays shoot out at dawn, the flowers fall to the ground and die.

How the Parijata tree came to earth

When the Ocean of Milk was churned, the Parijata tree was created. But Indra, the chief of the gods, thought it was far too beautiful for the Earth. Its bark is of gold and it is embellished with young sprouting leaves of a copper colour and its fruit stalks bear numerous clusters of fragrant fruit, he said eloquently, if rather inaccurately. Anyway, he took it to his heavenly garden Amaravati and there it grew as one of his five celestial trees, till Krishna brought it back to Earth.

How did Krishna bring it to Earth? In the days when the gods visited the Earth and sometimes even took human form, lived a divine sage called Narada Muni. Narada travelled frequently between Svargaloka where the gods lived and Earth. He was a mischievous sage who took great delight in creating problems for both gods and humans.

One day Narada Muni arrived in Dvaraka where the god Vishnu, who had been born on earth as Krishna, lived with his wives. Narada brought a single Parijata flower with him as a gift for Krishna.

"My Lord," he said, mischief hidden in his voice, "This flower is so beautiful that I thought you might like to give it to your wife Rukmini who so loves flowers."

Krishna was very pleased. "What a good idea, Muni. I don't think Rukmini has ever seen a Parijata flower before." He took the small orange and white blossom and went to Rukmini's chambers.

Narada saw his opportunity. He sped to the rooms of Krishna's other wife Satyabhama and, as he entered, he made his face mournful. Satyabhama looked concerned. "What troubles you, Muni?" she asked worriedly.

"My child", he answered sorrowfully, "You know how special you are to me. I had brought a Parijata flower from Indra's garden for Krishna. I told the lord to give it to his favourite wife. I thought you would enjoy the gift. But, alas, he has given it to Rukmini. "

Satyabhama had a short and explosive temper. "How dare he!" she cried angrily. "I won't let Rukmini have it. I'll go and . . . "

"Calm down, child," said Narada," "What will you do with a single flower? Now, if Krishna loved you he would bring the tree itself from Amaravati."

Satyabhama's face lit up. "How clever you are!" she exclaimed.

Narada bowed in acceptance of the compliment and Satyabhama left the room hurriedly.

In Krishna's palace was a room called The Chamber of Sorrow. Any wife who felt herself mistreated could retire to this room and her complaint would be heard. Satyabhama, her face like thunder, entered the room and sent her handmaiden to call Krishna.

As soon as Krishna walked through the doorway Satyabhama burst out weeping. "You love Rukmini more than me. Why did you give her the Parijata flower? I won't stay here any more", she wailed.

Krishna was taken aback. Too late, he saw the trap that he had fallen into. "My beloved, Narada Muni is . . ." he started to explain, but Satyabhama cut him short.

"No, no, I won't listen to any of your excuses. If you love me you will bring me the Parijata tree. Or I will stay in this room forever and refuse to eat."

Krishna saw no way out. "Very well", he gave in, "you shall have the tree."

He flew to Amaravati. But Narada had already been there. "I have heard that some thieves from Earth are coming to steal your Parijata tree, my Lord," he had whispered into Indra's ear.

Alarmed, Indra had sent his celestial guards to surround the garden. Krishna knew how dear the tree was to Indra and that he would not give it away readily. He stole into the grove at night. But the guards were too quick for him. He was captured and taken before the chief of gods.

"Krishna, you!" exclaimed Indra. "Why have you come to steal my tree?"

Krishna told him how he had been trapped by Sage Narada. "You know Satyabhama's temper", he said shrugging his shoulders. "I cannot return to Dvaraka without the tree. "

Indra laughed. "Wives!" He ordered the Parijata tree to be uprooted and given to Krishna immediately.

On his way back Krishna found himself in a greater dilemma. "If I give the tree to Satyabhama, Rukmini will demand another one. Where will I get that from? Oh dear."

Then he smiled to himself as he hit upon a solution.

Satyabhama was ecstatic when she saw Krishna and the tree. "Thank you, my Lord," she said flushed with happiness. She turned to order her handmaidens to take it away but Krishna said firmly. "I have brought the tree for you. But I will decide where it is to be planted. "

Clever Krishna! Both his wives had adjoining gardens. He planted the Parijata tree in such a way that while its trunk stood in Satyabhama's garden, its branches drooped into Rukmini's and she collected the flowers that fell every morning. And so Krishna kept both his wives happy and the Parijata tree came to Earth.

It is a small, quick growing deciduous tree. The leaves grow opposite each other and each large ovate leaf is dark green on its upper surface and light green and hairy below.

The seven petalled flowers come out in bunches of five at the side and ends of the branchlets. Each starlike creamy flower has an orange tube heart and sits in a pale green cup. The flowers open out in the evening permeating the air with a strong fragrance. They fall off at daybreak.

The fruit is larger than the flower, starting off as green, round and flat and turning brown and brittle just before it falls off. Each fruit has two seeds.

The leaves are so rough that they are used for polishing wood instead of fine sandpaper. The bark is used for tanning leather.

2

RED SILK COTTON TREE

Latin Names	*Bombax malabaricum,* *Salmalia malabarica*
English Name	*Red Silk Cotton Tree*
Indian Names	*Bengali : Shimul* *Gujarati : Raktashimul,* *Ratoshemalo, Sawar* *Hindi : Semul, Raktasimul* *Marathi : Sayar* *Malayalam : Ilavu* *Sanskrit : Yamadruma, Shalmali* *Telugu : Buraga, Salmali* *Tamil :Ilavam, Pulai*
Family	Bombacaceae

Bombax comes from Bombux which, in Greek, means silkworm. *Malabaricum* signifies that the tree came from the Malabar. Salmalia is a Latinized form of the Sanskrit Shalmali.

It is said that Pitamaha, the creator of the world, rested under the Semul after his labours were over. Its cuplike flowers are considered sacred to Shiva. When the tree is in full bloom it is compared to Lakshmi, the goddess of good fortune, standing with her arms out-stretched and a lit oil lamp on each palm.

Its Sanskrit name Yamadruma means Tree of the Infernal Regions, because though it makes a great show of its flowers, its fruit is not edible. Also, according to the *Mahabharata*, its thorns are used for torture in one of the seven hells.

15

This tree attracts the most birds of all the trees in India.

Why the Semul trunk has thorns
(An Oriya tribal legend)

The Raja of Judagarh village had two wives. But he was childless. He loved his wives dearly and did not want to marry again, but he had to have an heir to the kingdom. He issued a proclamation that whoever cured his wives of their infertility would be given half the village as his kingdom.

In the neighbouring village of Kanguda Dongar lived Kaliya Dano. He was known as a holy man but he was actually a demon who ate humans. Kaliya Dano sent word to the Raja of Judagarh that he could cure both wives. Accordingly, both were sent to him for treatment.

Kaliya Dano ate them up. Months passed. Messages were sent to Kaliya Dano asking him about the queens but Kaliya Dano pretended he was in meditation and did not reply. Finally the Raja of Judagarh took some men and went to Kanguda Dongar to bring back his wives.

Kaliya Dano saw the Raja approach the village. He fled to the forest behind the village. The Raja entered the hut and found it empty. He ordered his men to search and when he found a few bones and a ring that belonged to one of his wives he realized what had happened. In fury he ran to the forest to kill Kaliya Dano.

But the demon had, in desperation, climbed a tall tree. And, as he climbed, he pulled out all his sharp teeth and pushed them into the trunk so that no one could climb up after him. The Raja and his men tried to pull out the teeth but they were too deeply embedded. The Raja could not climb up and the demon would not come down. And there he perches to this day.

Why the Semul loses its leaves

In the heart of the Himalayas grew a large, evergreen Semul tree. It was greatly praised by travellers for they could rest in its leafy shade all the year round.

One day Narada Muni, the sage who delighted in confusion and misunderstanding between mortal and god, stopped by the tree.

"Mighty Semul", he said admiringly, "How is it that you never lose a leaf? Has Pavana, the God of the Wind, befriended you so that you are immune to his blasts?"

The Semul was arrogant in its splendour. "I don't need Pavana's protection or friendship. In fact he has often tried to harm me but my strength is greater than his. "

Narada was delighted at this opportunity to create more trouble. He went straight to Svargaloka where Pavana lived and bowed in mock distress.

"My Lord," he said dramatically, "Indra, the God of Rain, Yama, the Lord of Death, Kubera, the Keeper of Wealth, Varuna of the Sea, all these gods acknowledge you to be more powerful than them. Why then does the Semul tree belittle your power?"

Pavana flew into a rage. He swept into the Himalayas and soon came to the Semul tree standing green and proud.

"Semul!" Pavana shouted, "I have spared you these many centuries because my grandfather Brahma, the Creator, once rested in your shade. But now you have dared to insult me. I will make sure you never grow a single leaf again."

The tree replied with equal anger. "Do what you please, Pavana. I am not afraid of your wrath. "

Night fell. The Semul fell to thinking and realized that its arrogance was wrong. It decided to punish itself. It shed its leaves and broke most of its branches. Then it waited for Pavana.

Pavana was not long in coming. He had brought his army with him. Rain, sleet, hail, snow, thunder and lightning. Each soldier advanced angrily for the battle.

And then the Wind God stopped short. He saw the tree waiting humbly, denuded of all its glory, its head bent. His anger cooled. "I came to inflict this very punishment on you," he said. "But now that you have realised your mistake I am no longer angry with you." So saying Pavana returned to Svargaloka.

The Semul grew back its branches and leaves. But it remembers this lesson. Each year it drops its leaves voluntarily to remind itself never to be arrogant again.

Bhima's trick
(Mahabharata)

The Pandavas and their wife Draupadi had been exiled to the forest. During the day the brothers worked at hunting food, gathering fuel and clearing the forest. In the evening when they came back exhausted Draupadi gave each a massage to ease his tired limbs.

One day Bhima decided to trick Draupadi. He smuggled in a thick log of Semul wood to his room, put it on his bed and covered it with a sheet. He sent someone to tell Draupadi that she should massage him first as he had fever. In the meantime he hid outside and listened through the window.

An unsuspecting Draupadi came in. Without removing the sheet she started massaging the log of wood.

"Your body feels very hard today," she commented. "You must really be in pain with all those muscles knotted up."

Draupadi massaged the log for half an hour. "Is that enough? I must get the food ready," she asked. But there was no answer. Draupadi continued. After another half hour she asked tenderly, "You must be better now. Shall I stop?" When there was no answer she removed the sheet anxiously - and saw the log of wood.

Her hands sore, her back hurting, Draupadi grew angry. And since she could not see Bhima she vented her rage on the log.

"This is the last time that anyone will touch you with love", she exclaimed. "From today you will grow thorns." She stormed out of the room.

Bhima, listening outside, realized that he had better stay out of Draupadi's way for a little while till she saw the humour of the situation. He clambered in through the window, and picking up the log, took it to a clearing and planted it. There it grew into a tall Semul tree – but with thorns on its trunk.

It is a lofty, rapid growing and long-lived deciduous tree with wide-spreading branches growing in symmetrical whorls looking like outstretched arms. In fact, the tree looks like an upside down candelabrum. The bark of the young tree is green and its trunk is covered with sharp conical prickles. As it grows older the bark turns light grey.

The leaves are lance-shaped, set like the fingers of a hand, and fall off just before the tree flowers.

The flowers are mostly a brilliant pink but can be crimson, orange, yellow or a light scarlet. They are large, fleshy, faintly veined and with soft hair all over. They grow close to the branches.

The fruit is almost egg shaped. Inside it are small brown black seeds embedded in white cottonwool. When the pods burst open, the cotton wafts through the air.

Every part of the tree is valuable. The timber makes matchsticks and packing boxes. Fisherman use logs made from the trunk as floats for their nets. The cotton is called Indian Kapok and is used for stuffing pillows. The gum heals wounds and the young flowers are often cooked and eaten.

3

TAMARIND TREE

Latin Name	*Tamarindus indica*
English Name	*Tamarind Tree, Indian Date*
Indian Names	*Bengali : Tentul*
	Hindi : Imli
	Marathi : Amli, Chinch
	Sanskrit : Amlika
	Telugu : Chinta
	Tamil : Puli
Family	Leguminoseae

The name Tamarind comes from the Persian word Tamar-i-Hind or Date of India. The Sanskrit word Amlika means sour taste.

Common folklore has it that the Tamarind tree is the home of spirits that do not let anything under the tree survive. Accordingly travellers are advised not to sleep in its shade.

The most famous Tamarind tree in India is in Gwalior, where it stands over the tomb of Emperor Akbar's musician Tansen. The legend goes that all classical singers should eat some leaves of this tree to make their voices as sweet as his.

Why the leaves of the Tamarind are so small
(A Sambalpur tribal legend)

Long long ago when both gods and demons walked the earth, Bhasmasura was the chief of the Asura or demon army. He challenged Mahadeo or Shiva, the god of

destruction, to a duel. The winner, it was decided, would become the ruler of the Earth. Mahadeo took up the challenge. The two fought and Bhasmasura was wounded several times. He ran for his life, fleeing through the forest looking for a place to hide. Then he saw a Tamarind tree with huge spreading branches and giant leaves. He climbed up hastily and covered himself with the leaves. Mahadeo found that the demon had vanished. He looked everywhere and as he passed under the Tamarind tree Bhasmasura shifted nervously and the leaves rustled. Mahadeo looked up. He knew his enemy had been found but he couldn't see him. He tried with one eye, then with both but the leaves hid the demon from sight. Mahadeo's patience was exhausted. With a roar of rage he opened the magical third eye in the centre of his forehead. Each leaf disintegrated into small pieces. Mahadeo saw Bhasmasura and killed him. The Earth was saved from the demons, but the leaves of the Tamarind have always remained small.

Rama's house in the forest
(Ramayana)

King Dasharatha of Ayodhya reluctantly exiled his son Rama to the forest for fourteen years. Rama smiled and went obediently to his new home. With him went his wife Sita and his younger brother Lakshmana.

Rama and Lakshmana looked for that part of the forest where they might be the most comfortable. They built a small hut under the shade of the Imli tree. The tree had large leaves and these sheltered the hut from both sun and rain.

But Rama was not happy. One day he mused to Lakshmana, "My father has sent us to this forest to see how well we cope with hardship. I'm sure he never meant for us to shelter ourselves from all that the gods send us." Even before he had finished his sentence Lakshmana, who loved his brother dearly, understood his dilemma. He drew his bow and shot a series of small arrows into the branches of the Imli tree. The large leaves split into thin fringes which could not protect the princes from any of the elements, and so they have remained to this day.

The King and the drum

Once upon a time there lived a king of Central India. He was handsome but very vain. He looked at himself constantly, in mirrors, in pools of water, even in other people's eyes when they spoke to him. "I am the handsomest King on Earth", he said to his courtiers. He paid less attention to ruling his kingdom than he did to having his hair styled and his body oiled. As a result his people grew poorer and unhappier.

But the king did not care. "Why!" he boasted one day in court, "I am probably more handsome than all the gods."

Unfortunately for the king a particularly bad-tempered god happened to be flying by and was incensed at what he heard.

"Something will have to be done about this king." He searched in his mind for an appropriate punishment. Then his eyes fell upon a bull. "Horns!" The god clapped his hands with malicious glee. "I'll see how His Handsomeness likes himself with horns."

When the king awoke the next morning he followed his normal routine. First he drew his mirror out from under his pillow and gazed into it.

Suddenly the guards outside the king's chamber heard a loud shriek. They came rushing in to find the king sitting upright in bed with a large pillow on his head.

"Out. . . out. . ." he waved a trembling finger at them. As they backed away, he shouted after them, "Send for the royal barber immediately."

The royal barber was a cheeky talkative little man. He came in briskly.

"You're up early today, Your Majesty, but why the pil . . ."

The king broke in. "Stop your patter and come close to my bed".

As the surprised barber drew close, the king said in his most commanding voice, "Barber, I am about to show you something. But if you talk about it to a single living soul I will have you flogged and hanged." The king slowly removed the pillow from his head.

"Oh!" The barber clapped his hands to his mouth in horror.

"Well, don't just stand there", said the king impatiently. "Do something to cover them up."

The barber tugged the king's hair this way and that and managed to cover the horns partially. The king put his nightcap on to hide the rest. "Now go and tell the court I am unwell. I will not see anyone." He sat up and glared at the barber. "And remember my warning."

The barber fled. As soon as the door of the bedchamber closed he started laughing. The palace people stopped him and asked him the reason for his mirth but the barber only shook his head helplessly and ran laughing through the halls.

"I will die if I don't tell someone," he groaned. "My stomach is swelling with the secret."

He saw the Tamarind tree standing in the middle of the royal courtyard. He went up to it and whispered the secret to its trunk.

That night there was a fierce storm and the Tamarind tree was blown down. The king was informed through the door, for he would not see anyone, and he commanded the tree to be given to the royal musician. "Let him make a drum from the trunk of the Tamarind and play it outside my door. "

Soon the drum made of Tamarind wood was ready. The courtiers assembled outside the king's door and the musician began to play. But instead of the thum thum thum that everyone expected, the Tamarind drum intoned, "The Raja has horns on his head. The Raja has horns on his head." The court burst out laughing and the king cried with rage.

"I won't stay in the palace a moment longer," he shouted, "I'll go to the forest and live by myself." He tore the nightcap off his head and ran out of the palace, seizing the Tamarind drum on his way out.

The king lived for several years in the forest. He learnt about the beauty of the world around him. He learnt to care for creatures smaller than himself. He grew strong and wise and selfless. His only companion was the Tamarind drum and the drum, when he beat it, gave him all the advice and experience of the old tree. He learnt to play it so beautifully that even the spirits of the trees were charmed and they went to meet the god who had given him the horns.

"Forgive him", they pleaded. "He has changed. Remove his horns and give him back his kingdom."

The god waved his hands and the horns disappeared.

During the day the king went down to a forest pool to drink water. While cupping his hands he saw his reflection, and his lean, sun-tanned face looked back at him, without any horns! And, as he sat up in surprise, several horse-riders burst into the clearing and he saw his courtiers. They knelt before him. "Your Majesty, forgive us and come back. The kingdom needs you."

The king went back to his realm. He kept his Tamarind drum beside him always and he ruled wisely. And yes, the barber kept his head, but lost his job!

It is a large, handsome, evergreen tree with spreading branches. The trunk is thick and short and the bark rough, almost black, and covered with long cracks

Each graceful airy leaf is separated into ten or more pairs of fringed stems. They are a brilliant green when they first grow, gradually turning to a dusty dark green.

The three-petalled flowers are a pale yellow with red veins. The flowers cluster in small bunches round the leaves.

The fruits hang like long, thick, curved green beans and turn rust-coloured as they ripen. The seeds are dark brown and squarish.

The pulp of the fruit has a pleasant, tart taste and is used in curries and chutnies. It is also used to polish brass. The seeds are boiled and ground and used by the tribals as flour. The wood is used for agricultural implements and the leaves make a pretty yellow dye used on silk. Most parts of the tree are used in medicinal tonics. In World War II it was a major fuel for the gasogen units that powered Indian trucks.

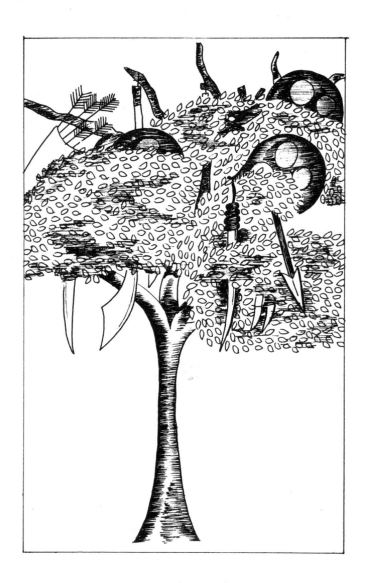

4

SHAMI TREE

Latin Name	*Prosopis spicigera*
English Name	None
Indian Names	*Hindi : Sami, Shami, Jand, Khejra*
	Kannada : Jambi
	Malayalam : Parampu
	Marathi : Shemri
	Punjabi : Jand
	Sanskrit : Shami
	Tamil : Perumbay
	Telugu : Jammi
Family	Leguminosae

Prosopis in Greek means obscure. *Spicigera* is taken from Adrian von der Spigel, a physician of the sixteenth century. The Sanskrit word Shami means pod.

The Vedas endowed the Shami tree with the property of containing fire. A Rigvedic legend says that Pururavas, the ancestor of the Lunar race of kings, which included the Kurus and Pandavas, generated the primeval fire by rubbing the two branches of the Shami and Ashvattha (*Ficus Religiosa*) trees together.

The Shami tree is held in reverence because Rama is supposed to have worshipped it before he set off with his army to recover Sita. Among the Rajputs, the chief or king goes in a procession to worship the tree on the tenth day of Dashehra and liberates a Jay, the sacred bird of Rama. In the Deccan, the Marathas shoot arrows at the Shami tree on the same day and put the falling leaves into their turbans.

It is also considered one of the abodes of Shiva. One of Shiva's names is Shamiroha or one who ascends the Shami tree.

The Bharvads of Gujarat make their marriage posts of the branches of this tree, believing it to be the home of the dreaded ghost Mamo or maternal uncle. In Punjab, when the bridegroom goes to fetch his bride home he cuts down a branch of this tree. The intention is to intimidate the evil spirits that abide there who are alleged to interfere with wedding rites.

How to marry a fourth time
(Matsya Purana)

From the Matsya Purana comes the ritual of marriage with the Shami tree. The ancient Brahmans permitted two marriages if a man did not have sons. But it was believed that a third marriage would cause the man to die shortly after. So if the man remained heirless he was married to a Shami tree. The ritual went like this: On Saturday and Sunday the Shami tree was worshipped as a representative of the Sun in union with his wife Chhaya. Raw sugar and boiled rice was offered to the tree. The man placed his hand on the trunk of the tree and said, "O Shami, created by Brahma Deva, that thou mayest protect me, O beneficient goddess, I prostrate myself before thee. O Daughter of the Sun, I worship thee. Mercifully preserve me, now that thou art come to be my wife. Thou were produced by Brahma Deva for the benefit of all living beings. Thou art the first born of trees who increased towards us the love of the gods. Ward off the dangers of a third marriage."

And to this the priest replied, "I will give to you of such a tribe, my daughter Arkakanya, the granddaughter of Sarla, the greatgranddaughter of Aditya, of the tribe of Kashyapa." After this curd, honey and sweets were offered. A veil was drawn between the bridegroom and the Shami tree and the marriage solemnized. The newly wedded husband garlanded the tree and the priest blessed them both. A thread was passed around the newly wedded couple and then tied to the groom's wrist and around a branch. The sacred fire was lit, Vishnu was worshipped and two cows given to the priest. After this ceremony the man was free to marry for the fourth time!

How the Pandava weapons were saved
(Mahabharata)

The Pandavas lost everything to the Kauravas in a game of dice between Yudhisthira and Duryodhana. The latter promised that he would return their kingdom to the Pandavas if they stayed in the forest for twelve years and incognito for another year. If they were recognized during that last year they would have to repeat their exile.

After twelve years in the forest, the Pandavas came to the kingdom of Virata and decided to disguise themselves and live in the court of the king there. Before they assumed their disguises, they took off their weapons, given to them by various gods, and hung them on a Shami tree. They found a corpse close by and suspended it from the branches, saying "this is the body of our mother. It must remain here for a year, after which we shall take it down and burn it." So, of course, no one dared to touch the weapons. When they returned

31

returned a year later still unrecognized, they found them safe in the branches of the Shami tree. Before taking them down, they worshipped the tree to thank it for keeping their weapons safe. When the Pandavas won the battle of Kurukshetra, the worship of the Shami tree on Dashehra day became a custom that is followed to this day.

It is a medium-sized, evergreen tree with a thin crown. The trunk rarely has straight sections. The branches are covered with conical prickles.

Each leaf is divided into small dark leaflets. The five-petalled flowers are small and yellow. The pods are long, slender and contract at intervals. They are filled with a dry sweetish pulp and seeds.

It is very valuable as a fodder tree.

5

TEMPLE TREE

Latin Name	*Plumeria (31 identified types, of which the most common are acutifolia, alba and rubra)*
English Names	*Pagoda Tree, Frangipani, Dead Man's Flower, Temple Tree, Graveyard Tree*
Indian Names	*Bengali : Golancha, Kathchampa* *Hindi : Champa, Gulachin* *Marathi : Khairchampa* *Sanskrit : Kshirachampa* *Tamil : Perungalli* *Telegu : Arhataganneru* *Urdu : Achin*
Family	Apocynaceae

The generic name *Plumeria* came from the French traveller and botanist Charles Plumier (1664-1706). It was mistakenly thought to have originated in China, which is why it was named Gulechin or Flower of China. The Sanskrit name Kshirachampa means the Milky Champa. Even the Frangipani is derived from the French *Frangipanier* which means coagulated milk. The second names are descriptive of the tree. *Acutifolia* is the variety with pointed leaves. Rubra is red and alba, white.

The ability of the tree to bloom even when it has been uprooted has made it a symbol of immortality. For this reason Buddhists and Muslims plant the tree next

to the tombs of their dead. In fact, images of the Buddha are carved from the wood of this tree.

The Hindus consider it one of the holiest trees and plant it near temples with the flowers being offered to the deity. The tree is considered sacred to Kamadeva, the God of Love, and it is inauspicious to cut it.

It was Mughal Emperor Jahangir's favourite flower. He wrote, "It is a flower of increasingly sweet fragrance; it has the shape of a saffron flower but is yellow inclining to white. The tree is very symmetrical and large, full of branches, and is shady. When in flower one tree will perfume a garden."

The Anglo-Indian phrase," to shake the Pagoda tree" was slang used by British adventurers to express the openings to rapid fortune which once existed in India.

The seven princes

Once upon a time lived a king who had two wives. The older wife was scheming and greedy. The younger wife was soft, gentle and beautiful, but alas, she was mute.

The older wife could not bear children. When she heard that the younger queen was to have a child she was bitterly jealous and afraid of losing her position. She made up her mind that the child would not be allowed to live.

When the time came for the child to be born, the older queen put her plan into action. She sent for the king. "My Lord," she said in an agitated voice, "I have just heard that dacoits are harassing your subjects living on the borders of the kingdom. It is your duty to save them."

The king did not want to leave the younger queen, but the older one assured him that every care would be taken. He rode away with his army and soon after the queen gave birth to a son. The older queen did not permit any attendants in the room when the child was born.

She snatched up the child and stuffed him in a basket of old clothes. Taking him outside the palace wall, she killed and buried him, then hurried back inside and put a monkey in the child's cradle.

The king returned without having found any dacoits. The older queen met him at the door of the palace and, before he could scold her for having sent him off on a false report, she started weeping and wringing her hands. "Your Majesty, you are ruined! The younger queen has given birth to a monkey."

The king was taken aback. He strode into the younger queen's chamber and saw the monkey in the royal cradle. He turned to the queen and saw her tremble, her eyes full of tears. The king loved the younger queen dearly and seeing her pathetic condition, he controlled his anger.

In the following years the younger queen gave birth to seven sons and a daughter. Each time, the older queen found a pretext to send the king away and each time she substituted a monkey for the baby. The eight children were killed and buried outside the palace wall.

The king grew more and more unhappy. He sent for his astrologers and wise men and they were equally perplexed at the strange births in the palace. The malicious older queen never lost an opportunity to poison the king's mind. "Your younger queen brings you bad luck", she whispered constantly. "You will be laughed at by your people as the father of monkeys." Finally she persuaded the king to banish the younger queen from the palace.

The innocent younger queen was thrown into a little hut near the palace wall and there she lived quietly. The king had a gate opened on the other side and he rode through that so that he would never have to see his younger wife.

A few years passed. Outside the palace wall grew seven handsome trees with beautiful, fragrant flowers like golden crowns. Near them grew a smaller delicate tree. The people of the kingdom had never seen trees of their magnificence. They named the large trees Champa and the little one Parul.

The fame of the trees spread throughout the kingdom. It became known that no one could pluck the flowers except the younger queen. And she did not have to pluck them at all, for when she came out of her hut, the flower-laden branches drooped and scattered their blossoms at her feet.

The king rarely left his palace now. The years had not been kind to him and he missed his younger wife desperately. He heard his courtiers talk of these trees and ordered the royal gardener to fetch him some Champa blossoms. But when the gardener approached the trees he heard the small one call out. "Brothers, shall we give our flowers to the king's gardener?" "No. Let the king come himself", answered the larger trees in unison.

The gardener returned empty handed and told the king what he had heard. The king, naturally, did not believe him. He sent his minister to fetch the flowers. The minister returned with the same tale. Astonished, the king decided to go and see these extraordinary trees for himself.

The older queen turned pale. She alone knew the truth and she realised the danger she was in. She tried to stop the king. But he was determined that both of them should see the trees.

As soon as the trees saw the older queen their branches drew back sharply. "Murderer!" came a single throated cry. The king came up to tnem and the branches nuzzled his ears while their soft voices rustled, "Bring our mother here."

"Who is your mother?" asked the puzzled king.

"Your younger queen", the little tree replied.

The king went into the hut of his younger queen and brought her out. As she neared the Champa tree their branches bent low and all their creamy yellow flowers cascaded into her hair and lap making her look radiant.

The older queen broke down and confessed her evil deeds. She was banished from the kingdom immediately. The happy king brought his younger queen back to the palace. The Champa and Parul trees were brought into the queen's garden and both the king and queen treated them like their children for the rest of their lives.

It is a quick-growing, medium-sized, deciduous tree. The bark is a smooth grey and the branches taper only slightly at the ends. If the bark is pierced a white milky juice flows out. When it is leafless, its pale, blunt swollen trunk and branches appear ugly and gouty. But when the leaves and flowers appear it is one of the most beautiful trees of the garden.

The stiff leaves are large, almost a foot long and taper at the ends or have a rounded apex depending on the variety. They grow in spirals at the ends of branches.

Tufts of creamy flowers appear in the middle of the cluster of leaves at the end of branchlets, five-petalled, large and waxy. The Alba variety is white with a sun yellow throat. The Rubra has deep pink and white petals.

The bark and sap are used for medicine, specially as a relief for rheumatism. In Goa the leaves are tied round coconut trees to protect them from beetles.

6

FLAME OF THE FOREST

Latin Name	*Butea monosperma,* *Butea frondosa*
English Names	*Flame of the Forest, Parrot Tree*
Indian Names :	*Bengali : Palash* *Hindi : Dhak, Palasa* *Malayalam : Brahmavriksham,* *Palasi* *Marathi : Kakracha, Palas, Paras* *Sanskrit : Kimsuka* *Tamil : Parasu* *Telugu : Moduga*
Family	Leguminosae

The name *Butea* was given in honour of a patron of botany, John Stuart (1713-92), the Earl of Bute. *Monosperma* means one seeded and *frondosa*, leafy. The Sanskrit word Kimsuka means "like a parrot" or "what brightness!" Palasha means both leaf and beauty in Sanskrit. The older name of the tree, Parna, again means leaf.

Mentioned frequently in the Vedas, its trifoliate leaves represent the Hindu Triad, with Brahma on the left, Vishnu in the middle and Shiva on the right. When a boy becomes a Sadhu he is given a Palasa leaf to eat and his staff is made of Palasa wood. The flowers of the Palasa are used to make a bright yellow or deep orange red impermanent dye. Devotees of Shiva and Vishnu paint their foreheads with it. In the *Mahabharata*, Sage Jamadagni performs a sacrifice to the gods in

Palasvana or the Palasa tree grove, a ceremony attended by all the rivers.

The tree in full bloom looks like fire on the horizon. In his *Ritusamhara*, Kalidasa describes the jungles of Dhak trees as resembling a blazing fire, making the earth look like a newly-wed bride with red garments. Poet Amir Khusrau compared the flowers to a lion's blood-stained claws.

The Palasa is considered sacred to the Moon. A falcon dipped its feathers in Soma or the drink of the gods, supposed to be made on or originating from the moon. One feather floated down to Earth and this became the Palasa tree.

The Buddhists also revere it for legend has it that Queen Mahamaya seized a branch of the Palasa tree at the very moment of the birth of her son Gautama Buddha.

A Hindu superstition has it that if the root of a Palasa tree is collected when the Ashvini constellation rules the season (mid-September to mid-October) and tied to a man's arm, any woman he touches will fall in love with him.

The curious formation of its flowers is the subject of many riddles in Bihar. One of them is:

An Elephant Tusk
But not a Tusk
The Body of a Monk
But not a Monk
The Head of a Crow
But not a Crow
But a Parakeet.

The dark glossy black calyx is the head of the crow. The petals are the colour of a monk's robe. The prominent stamen is the tusk. And the keel is the beak of the parakeet.

But, for all their beauty, the flowers are scentless. In the old books, a person with beauty but without moral or intellectual qualities is referred to as a human Palasa.

How the Palasa came to earth

(An early Indo-Aryan tale)

One day Indra, the chief of the gods, felt a great thirst. The gods of his court asked the goddess Gayatri to go to the celestial mountain Mujavana where the Soma creeper grew and bring it back so that Indra would then have an uninterrupted supply of Soma forever after.

Gayatri disguised herself as an eagle. She flew to the mountain and found it guarded by the sentries of the Moon. She swooped down and, in a trice, seized the creeper in her beak. Before the startled sentries could do anything she flew away, screeching triumphantly.

One of the sentries, Krishanu, let fly an arrow at the bird. The arrow missed Gayatri but struck the vine. One of the leaves fell off and it fell to Earth and grew into the Palasa tree.

The two lovers

(A Koraput tribal legend)

Long ago, the Pengu, Muria and Bhattra tribes had a leader called Chaitu Bhattra. Chaitu Bhattra's daughter was married against her wishes. Soon after her marriage she fell in love with a dark, handsome Muria boy and the two used to meet secretly.

42

The couple were seen by the villagers who told the husband about his wife's secret meetings. The husband wanted proof for himself and he set a trap for his wife. One day he told Chaitu Bhattra's daughter, "Wife, I am going to my sister's house in the next village. I will return in a few days." He pretended not to see the smile that flowered on her face. Tying his clothes together, he took his staff and set out.

But he only went as far as the forest. He hid during the day and returned home late at night. He found the Muria boy in his hut. The husband was furious and beat the pair with his stick till they were dead. Then he took their corpses out and threw them in the forest.

Blood from both the bodies flowed and joined into a single stream. From this stream grew a tree. The flowers were red for the girl and black for the boy. And this was the first Parsa or Palasa tree.

It is a medium-sized, deciduous tree with a crooked trunk and branches. The bark is rough and greyish. The branches are velvety and dark olive green in colour.

The large trifoliate leaves are stiff, velvety to begin with and leathery later, and a pale bronze green in colour. When the leaves are shed the flowers come out and these transform the appearance of the tree.

The flowers grow in groups of three. Each flower is a flamelike orange-scarlet. Standing in stiff clusters each blossom is more than two inches long and each of the five petals is soft and covered with fine hair so that it glistens in the sunlight. The petals curve backwards and one of them forms an unusual beak-shaped keel which gives the tree its name of Parrot Tree or Totaphul.

The fruit is a flat, long pod narrowing at the tip. From a pale green it turns yellow-brown and contains only one seed.

The most useful product is the red astringent gum from the stems which is used for tanning leather. The Lac insect lives in the Palasa trees and its lacquer is used as sealing wax and in

43

dyes. The leaves make plates and strangely enough, at one stage, were used as umbrellas! They also make fodder for cattle. The root fibres make rope. Farmers burn the branches and mix the ash with cowdung to spread on rice fields as fertilizer. The wood lasts well under water, so makes waterscoops.

7

BANANA

Latin Names	*Musa paradisiaca* *Musa sapientum*
English Names	*Banana, Plantain, Apple of* *Paradise, Adam's Apple*
Indian Names	*Bengali : Kala* *Hindi : Kela, Kadali* *Kannada : Bale* *Malayalam : Vazha* *Sanskrit : Mocha* *Tamil : Vazhai* *Telugu : Arati*
Family	Musaceae

Musa is named after Antonio Musa, physician to Octavius Augustus Caesar (63-14 B.C.). *Paradisiaca* means Paradise, of which it is supposed to have been the first inhabitant. It is said that this tree flourished in the Garden of Eden and its leaves were the first garments of Adam and Eve. The Sanskrit word *Mocha* means juicy and also ascetic or one who has abandoned worldly passions. *Sapientum*, strangely enough, means wise or sage. The Hindi word Kela means shaking, trembling. The name Kadali means flag or banner.

The botanist, Rumphuis, writes that the banana came from East India, growing first on either side of the Ganges river, and from there it went to Persia, Syria, Arabia and Egypt. Buddhist sculptures show banana leaves and a drink called Mochapana is mentioned in the Buddhist book of monastic rules.

According to legend, the Banana fertilizes itself without cross pollination. So it is regarded as an incarnation of the goddess Parvati. In eastern India, marriage podiums have Banana stalks at the corners. In the Western Ghats, the Banana tree is believed to be the Goddess Nanda Devi. Her images are carved out of the stalk and, in the month of Kartika, floated down the river. In the *Mahabharata*, Kadalivana or the Banana garden on the banks of Kuberapushkarni is the home of the monkey god, Hanuman.

The Banana plant is considered sacred to the nine forms of the Hindu goddess Kali. In Bengal marriages are performed under it and it is worshipped in the month of Sravan (July-August). A saying in Bengali goes:

Kala lagiye na keto pat
Tatei kapad tatei bhat.

(Do not destroy the leaves of a planted banana,
You will get both your food and cloth.)

Since the plant is cut after the fruit is harvested, it has become a folk simile of the bad man destroyed by the fruit of his own deeds.

Why the Banana tree is short-lived
(A Gadaba tribal legend)

Mango, Tamarind, Plantain, Fig and Black Plum were five dancing sisters who decided to get married. They went from village to village looking for husbands but no one would marry them. The god Ispur Mahaprabhu thought, "If I leave these sisters unmarried, it will be a sin".

47

So he asked the five sisters what they wanted. Four of them said together, "We want husbands and many, many children". But pretty Plantain said, "I don't want a husband at all. As for children, not very many, for then I shall lose my looks and grow old soon".

The four girls were given husbands. The plantain, only children. Soon they had as many children as the hair on their heads. The husbands took fright at their large families and ran away. The mothers too tried to run away. But their children caught them and would not let them go. In desperation the sisters prayed to Mahaprabhu, "Help us or we shall be destroyed by our children!"

Mahaprabhu turned the girls into trees. Their hair became branches and the children fruit. "What will you do for husbands?" asked Mahaprabhu.

"Anyone who climbs our branches will be our husband", replied four of the sisters. So men became the husbands of these trees. But the Plantain refused a husband and, because men keep the trees young with their love, the Plantain has only a few children and matures in one year.

The story of Kadaligarbha

(Kathasaritsagara)

Near the city of Ikshumati was a great forest. In it lived a hermit called Mankanaka. He fell in love with the celestial maiden Menaka. To him was born a beautiful daughter. And since she was born inside a Plantain tree, she was named Kadaligarbha, that is, from the womb of the Plantain. She lived with the saint in the forest.

48

One day the king of Madhyadesha, Dhridhavarman, passed the hermitage. He saw Kadaligarbha and was captivated by her beauty. He bowed before her father and asked for her hand.

All the nymphs of heaven came for Menaka's daughter's wedding. As Kadaligarbha left with her husband, the maidens gave some mustard seeds to her saying, "Sow these along the path that takes you to the city. If your husband should scorn you, and you should want to come back, you will be able to recognize the path by these." Kadaligarbha scattered the seed all the way to her new palace.

Dhridhavarman loved his new bride deeply and spent all his time with her. The other wives grew jealous. His principal wife sent her maid to call a female ascetic who knew magic.

"Get rid of Kadaligarbha", she whispered, "And I shall reward you handsomely."

The female ascetic answered glibly, "Certainly, Queen. My magic shall not fail."

But when the ascetic returned home, she thought about the promise that she had so rashly made. The truth was that she knew no magic at all. Afraid, she went to her friend, the barber.

The old and cunning barber thought that this would be a good way to become rich for the rest of his life. "But we must not kill her", he mused to the ascetic. "Her father is a sage and will surely find out. We must hide Kadaligarbha. Thus we shall become confidantes of the queen and obtain wealth. And in time we can restore her to the king so that he too will be grateful and give us more wealth. "

The barber sent the ascetic to instruct the queen that an old servant should tell the king everyday that his wife Kadaligarbha was a witch. As the king's fears grew, one night the servant should put severed hands and legs in Kadaligarbha's chambers. This was done. The king abandoned Kadaligarbha and she left the palace.

She found her way back to her father's hermitage following the path of the mustard seeds that had sprung up. Mankanaka was surprised to see her. Sobbing, she told him the story. He took her back to the palace and related the whole story to the king.

The barber had taken away the sacks of gold given to him by the queen. Now he heard that the sage Mankanaka had come to the palace. In a flash he presented himself to the king. "I was just coming to tell you, sire. . . " the rogue began smoothly and went on to betray the queen. Kadaligarbha was taken back, the queen was expelled from the palace and the crafty barber was rewarded a second time over for his honesty!

Although usually called a tree, the banana is really an outsize, broad-leafed, perennial, herbaceous plant. It grows quickly, giving fruit in a year. What is called the trunk is really the pseudostem, the real one being underground. The deep green leaves are enormous but so soft that they are torn easily by strong winds or storms. Each leaf emerges tightly rolled round its own midrib and then slowly opens out. The leaves that emerge later are shorter, the very last one being very short and hanging protectively over the flowerbud.

The fruit, the bananas, are like long, fat fingers, in bunches of twelve each. Each plant can yield several bunches. The skin of the fruit is thick and green when it is unripe, changing to yellow, and even a light pink in some varieties, as it ripens. It is seedless and the pulp is sweet.

The banana contains iron, minerals, phosphorus and vitamins. It is one of the most important energy-giving foods and is usually the first solid food given to a baby as it is easy to digest. Unripe bananas are used as vegetables. The leaves make plates. The wild banana plant is used to border crop fields as it keeps away termites.

8

BANYAN TREE

Latin Name	*Ficus benghalensis linn*
English Name	*Banyan Tree*
Indian Names	*Bengali : Bot*
	Gujarati : Vad
	Hindi : Bar, Bargad
	Malayalam : Peral
	Marathi : Vad
	Sanskrit : Vata
	Tamil : Ala
	Telegu : Peddamari
Family	Moraceae

The name Banyan is said to have been given by the British to a tree under which Banias or Hindu merchants assembled for business and worship. *Ficus* means fig and *Benghalensis* is of or pertaining to Bengal. The Sanskrit word Vata means to surround or encompass.

The Banyan, the Ganges and the Himalayas, these three symbolize the image of India. To most Indians the tree is sacred and only in the most dire circumstances, a famine for instance, will its leaves be plucked for cattle fodder.

The tree symbolizes all three gods of the Hindu Triad. Vishnu is the bark, Brahma, the roots, and Shiva, the branches. Another name for Kubera, the treasure-keeper of the gods, is Vatashraya, one who lives in the Banyan tree. According to tradition it is visited by the goddess Lakshmi on Sundays.

The Puranas tell the story of Savitri who lost her husband a year after her marriage. He died under a Banyan tree and, by worshipping this tree, Savitri succeeded in bringing him to life again. This legend has given rise to a special puja that is done on Vat Savitri day when women fast and go round the Banyan tree.

Banyan trees were regarded as symbols of fertility, venerated by those who wanted children. The *Mahabharata* tells of a mother and daughter who embraced two Banyan trees and became the mothers of Sage Vishvamitra and Sage Jamadagni.

In the Hattipala Jataka of the Buddhists is the story of the woman with seven sons who said that she prayed to the deity of the Banyan tree who blessed her with sons.

A pilgrimage to one of the main Banyan trees is considered the equivalent of twelve years of sacrifice and it is believed that one who anoints himself with the ashes of any part of this tree becomes sin-free.

In Hindu mythology, Vishnu was born under its shade. One of the earliest forms of Indian sculpture is the Kalpavriksha or Wish-granting tree of Besnagar, now in the Indian Museum, Calcutta. It has been identified by Ananda Coommaraswami as a Banyan tree. The Aryans portrayed Indra as sitting with his queen shaded by a Banyan from whose branches people gathered jewels, clothes, food and drink. Also called the Agastyavata, it symbolizes immortality. When the whole world was flooded during the Great Deluge, a leaf of the Banyan tree cradled Balmukunda safely through the waters.

How Amba took the tree from Vasuki

(A Bhil legend from Rajasthan)

Vasuki was the great Serpent Lord of Patalaloka, the World of the Nether Regions. In his magnificent garden was a giant Banyan tree.

The goddess of Earth, Amba, dreamt of this tree. Impressed by its grandeur, she wanted to bring it to Earth. But she could not find a way to enter Patalaloka.

She asked all the birds and animals. But no one had ever been and returned from there. Of all the insects only the beetles knew, for they went up and down constantly, burrowing their way through the worlds. But they had been sworn to secrecy. Amba cajoled and commanded but the beetle king would not divulge his secret. So she had him thrown in a cauldron of boiling oil. Sure enough, the beetle king talked.

Amba arrived in the garden of Vasuki. She started walking round the tree to encircle it with her magic and take it away when Vasuki saw her. A flame shot out of his eyes and Amba fell dead to the ground.

The divine Mahadeva and Parvati were also walking about in this wondrous garden of Vasuki's when they came across the body of Amba. Parvati was shocked and upset. She asked Mahadeva what had happened and what could be done about Amba. Mahadeva knew what had happened, for Mahadeva knew everything, but he ignored Parvati's frantic questions.

Parvati saw Mahadeva's indifference. Amba was an incarnation of Parvati herself and so she was even more anguished. She decided to punish Mahadeva and disappeared.

"Come back, Parvati", called Mahadeva. But the goddess sulked and refused to return. Finally Mahadeva gave in. He brought Amba back to life.

But Amba was angry and so was Parvati. "One more boon. Only then will I return", said Parvati. What could Mahadeva do? He agreed to grant one wish of Amba's. "I want revenge on Vasuki."

Vasuki, the Snake Lord, had a thousand heads. Amba cut off all his heads but one and while the blood streamed from the wounds, she took the Banyan tree to Earth.

How the Banyan tree nourished man
(A tribal tale from Ganjam district)

Nirantali, the first keeper of the world, was sent by the gods to live in Saphaganna. She brought with her some Banyan seeds, wrapped in leaves.

When the Earth and the clouds were ready, men were born. Both the Sun and the Moon shone upon them and they felt very hot all the time. They had no shade for their mud houses. So they took the Banyan seeds from Nirantali and planted them. These grew into slender trees with very tiny leaves that provided no shade at all.

Nirantali tugged and pulled at the leaves till they were large. Then she stretched the branches till they came down to the Earth. And so shade was provided.

But men still did not have proper food to eat. So Nirantali told the Banyan tree, "Feed men with your milk". The banyan replied, "I have only blood in my body. Where should I get the milk from?" Nirantali swung her axe, hit the trunk of the tree and said, "Let

56

milk flow". And so it did and men lived on it till grain came to the world.

The Banyan tree has been described as the most astounding piece of vegetation on the face of this earth. It is an evergreen tree which grows to about one hundred feet in height. It sends down roots from its branches and these enter the ground and become trunks. At first the roots are slender but as soon as they anchor themselves they become thick pillars that bear the weight of the heaviest branches.

The leaves are broadly oval, deep green above and pale green underneath. They are smooth and shiny when young, and stiff and leathery when old. If broken they ooze a milky white fluid.

The flowers and fruit are inconspicuous. The fruit is a green hard fig that emerges from the angle between the leafstalk and the branch and turns red and soft as it matures. The fruit is eaten by almost all birds.

How wide does a Banyan grow? The tree in Chicholi, Hoshangabad, is an acre and a half wide. In Chunchanakuppe, near Bangalore, the tree, said to be five centuries old, is almost three acres wide. From a seed planted in 1792 the tree at the Botanical Gardens in Sibpur, Calcutta, has grown to a size where its trunk is larger than 51 feet in girth and it has over a thousand aerial branches, its canopy covering four acres. The tree in Satara was last measured in 1882 when its circumference was 483 metres.

9

JUJUBE TREE

Latin Name	*Zizyphus jujube*
English Names	*Chinese Date, Chinese Fig, Jujube Tree*
Indian Names	*Bengali : Kul* *Hindi : Ber* *Marathi : Bor* *Malyalam : Ilantai* *Sanskrit : Badara, Badari* *Telugu : Reegu* *Tamil : Elandai*
Family	Rhamnaceae

Zizyphus comes from the Arabic word *Zizouf* which means nut-bearing lotus. *Zizyphon* is Greek for *jujube* or edible plum-like fruit. *Zizyphwn*, the Latin word, means the same thing.

A grove of Badari trees at the foot of the Himalayas was chosen for the hermitage of the two great saints, Nara and Narayana, the latter being an incarnation of Vishnu. The site, Badrinath, is a sacred pilgrimage centre for the Hindus.

The Ber tree is a part of folklore in north India, especially the Punjab. It is considered unlucky to plant it within the house, as it is supposed to make the inhabitants quarrel. The Dukhbhanjani or sorrow-removing tree of the Golden Temple in Amritsar is revered by the Sikhs.

Apparently the formal cultivation of this tree began when a Muslim contractor won an Inam or royal award when he presented a hybrid variety of the fruit to Raja Raghoji Bhonsale II of Ahmadnagar.

Why the Ber is sturdy
(Ramayana)

Sita had disappeared from the forest. Rama and Lakshmana hunted anxiously for her but they did not know which direction to take. As they searched, they heard a small ill-kempt Ber tree call out to them.

"Rama, my Lord, I saw Sita being carried away. She passed by me and I caught her garment with all my strength to stop her. But my branches are weak. See, I only succeeded in tearing her garment and a scrap of her dress is still clinging to my thorns." The tree drooped in shame.

But Rama was pleased and blessed the tree for its courage. "Ber tree, for this act, you will achieve immortality. Even when you are hacked down to your roots by men, but a single root of yours remaining in the ground will bring you back to life again. "

Shabari and the half-eaten fruit
(Kamban Ramayana)

Malini was the daughter of the Gandharva king Chitravacha. For her unfaithfulness to her husband, Vitihotra, she was cursed to be born in a tribe of forest dwellers. Malini wept and her husband relented slightly.

"Vishnu, as Rama, will take your curse away."

Malini was reborn as Shabari near the forest hermitage of Sage Matanga. She served his devotees and spent her days awaiting the arrival of Rama.

While hunting for Sita, Rama and Lakshmana came across her humble dwelling. Shabari was overjoyed at this honour and rushed inside her hut to find something to offer the royal visitors. But she had nothing except a few Ber berries from a tree growing near the hut.

Shabari wanted to make sure that Rama only ate the sweet berries. So she bit into each fruit, and if it turned out sweet she gave it to either brother. The sour ones she threw away. Rama ate each fruit given to him for he saw the love and devotion that had made this illiterate woman taste the berries. But the fastidious Lakshmana threw the bitten fruit away. It is said that the life-giving herb Sanjivani grew out of the fruit that he threw away and later, when he was dying, this herb saved his life.

As for Shabari, as soon as Rama blessed her for her devotion, she was transformed into Malini, the Gandharva maiden. All at once, her husband appeared at her side and after saluting Rama, Vitihotra took his wife away to the city of the Gandharvas in the sky.

The sorrow remover
(A legend from the Punjab)

Duli Chand, a nobleman of the town Patti, had four married daughters and one unmarried one. For years he and his wife had prayed for a son and he had grown embittered with God for not giving him one.

One day the five sisters went on a picnic and they saw some Sadhus singing devotional songs. The youngest sister was so moved that she removed her jewellery and distributed it among the Sadhus.

When the sisters came home, Duli Chand saw the bare arms and neck of his youngest daughter and was told that she had given away her jewels to men of god. Infuriated, the father summoned all five daughters and asked,"Who cherishes and protects you? Who gives you food, clothes and jewellery?" The four elder sisters answered promptly. "You, Father." But the youngest looked at the sky and said. "God is my protector."

Duli Chand's anger increased. He found a deformed leper and married the youngest, Bibi Rajani, to him. "I will see how God protects you now", he said and threw the couple out of his house.

Bibi Rajani went from village to village begging for food for her husband and herself. She took her husband to each temple on pilgrimage. While on their travels, they came to Amritsar. Bibi Rajani made her husband comfortable under a Ber tree on the bank of a waterhole and then went away to beg for the day's food.

The leper sat under the tree and watched the pool of water. He saw the miracle of jet black crows diving into the water to cool off and emerging a glistening white. He dragged himself to the edge of the water and timidly dipped his body in. With his little finger, he held on to a branch of the Ber tree. He was cured immediately, his body coming out whole from the pool.

When his wife returned she did not recognize her husband. She refused to believe that the healthy stranger standing in front of her was a leper that had been cured by the miracle water. Both of them went before the Sikh Guru Ramdass.

Guru Ramdass took them back to the pool. There he showed Bibi Rajani her husband's leprous little finger which had held on to the Ber tree. He dipped the finger in the pool and it too came out whole.

A tank was built around this pool and it has, till today, the reputation for miraculous healing. The Ber tree on its bank is the Dukhbhanjani Beri.

It is a small to medium-sized evergreen tree with thin vine-like scraggly zigzag branches. The bark is a cracked, thick, dark grey. The branches droop down and have sharp thorns growing in pairs at the base of the leafstalks.

The leaves are small and far between. They are ovate, dark green on the upper surface and covered with soft white hair on the underside.

The flowers are tiny stars, pale greenish yellow clusters. The fruit is roughly egg-shaped, ranging from small red berries to the longer yellow-green cultivated variety. The skin is hard and thin and each berry has one stony seed.

The Ber is an excellent fuel and fodder tree. Being hardy it can withstand drought and frost and is ideal for barren areas. The fruit is rich in vitamins and is eaten, preserved or made into sherbet.

10

COCONUT PALM

Latin Name	*Cocos nucifera*
English Name	*Coconut Palm*
Indian Names	*Bengali : Dab, Narkol*
	Hindi : Narial, Khopra
	Malayalam : Thenna, Tenga,
	Thengu
	Marathi : Naral
	Sanskrit : Narikela, Narikera,
	Suphala
	Telugu : Narikelamu, Tenkai
	Tamil : Tennaimaram
Family	Arecaceae/Palmae

Cocos means grimace in Portuguese as the fruit is said to resemble a monkey's head and the three holes at the nut's base give it the look of a grinning face. *Nucifera* means nut bearing. The Sanskrit word *Narikela* comes from the root *Narik* which means with water.

On the Hindu New Year it is considered auspicious to see a coconut immediately one's eyes open. The Bengalis believe that a coconut has eyes and will never fall on the head of a passer-by. In Gujarat it is a family god. The Muslims of Deccan India throw cut coconut and lime over the heads of bridegrooms to scare away evil spirits. In western India coconuts are thrown into the sea at the close of the monsoons to satiate and pacify the waters.

Because a coconut resembles a human head, it was offered to Goddess Bhadrakali instead of a human sacrifice.

How the Coconut got its face
(A folktale from Kerala)

A young man from Kerala, born into a fisherman's family, did not know how to catch fish. He tried all the ways, with poles and nets, but he never caught any fish and he got poorer and hungrier. Everybody in his village laughed at him.

So he decided to learn some magic. He went to a teacher of magic and learnt how to remove his head from his body.

When the beach was deserted in the evenings, when all the fishermen had returned to their villages with their daily catch, he would come to the beach and, in a secluded corner, take off his head from his trunk and dive into the water. The fish had never seen such a strange sight and they always clustered round. All the small fish entered his body through his neck. The man would then swim ashore, take the fish out, and replace his head. He would go back to his village and show the villagers all the fish that he had caught.

He told no one his secret. The villagers who saw no poles or nets in his hut nor caught sight of him at the beach grew exceedingly curious. One day a little boy followed him to the shore. He saw him take off his head and dive into the water. The little boy darted forward and snatching the head, ran away. After a few yards he found it too heavy and threw it into a bush.

The man came out of the water and could not find his head. He searched all over and then, because his magic was running out, he threw himself back into the sea and became a fish.

The little boy brought all the villagers to show them the miracle of the head. But when they came to the bush at the side of sea, they found that it had already grown into a tall and slender palm with nuts on it . Each nut had the man's face on it. And thus the coconut tree was created.

How the Coconut came to earth

Trishanku was a famous king of the Solar dynasty. He was a pious ruler, renowned for his devotion to the gods. Trishanku had only one desire. He did not want to wait till he died and his soul went to heaven. He wanted to go there with his mortal body intact.

There was a great famine in the country. Sage Vishvamitra and his family lived in a forest of the kingdom. The Sage had gone away to another country and his family was starving. Trisanku helped them with food.

When Vishvamitra returned to his hermitage and heard of Trisankhu's deed, he promised to help the king achieve his desire. He started a Yagna or sacrifice to the gods. As the fire and the prayers grew in strength Trisanku started rising off the ground. Soon he was far above the Earth, above the clouds, and had neared the gates of Svargaloka where the gods lived.

As soon as the gods saw a mortal at the gates, they ran complaining to their king, Indra. Indra, angry at the daring of Trisanku, pushed the king down again.

As Trisanku fell he cried out in fear to Vishvamitra. The sage looked up and saw the unfortunate king falling fast through the sky. His anger knew no bounds. He shouted, "Let Trisanku stay where he is".

Trisanku stopped in mid-air. But the sage knew that the king would only be able to stay aloft for a little while and soon the magic chant would wear off. So he held him up with a long pole.

In time this pole became the trunk of the Coconut tree and Trisanku's head became the coconut fruit.

It is a tall tree with a straight, uniformly thick and circled trunk and a crown of large feather-like fronds. The leaves are long and divided into hundreds of sword-shaped leaflets fixed on a stout stem. Each leaflet is shiny green and leathery.

The yellowish orange flowers grow on a branched stalk that starts from the point the leaves join the trunk.

The coconut fruit is large and three-sided. It has a hard green coat which turns brown when ripe. Inside a thick layer of stout fibre surrounds a hard shell. This contains a thick coating of soft milky white flesh and sweet water.

This palm is extremely useful. The leaves are used for roof thatching, the trunk for small boats. The sap of the tree yields a juice called Toddy which is made into alcohol and also sugar. Brooms are made from the leaf ribs. The fibre from the husk is called coir and is used for ropes, carpets and stuffing. The shell is used for fuel and for scoops. It is also burnt and made into black paint. The kernel or copra is eaten fresh or used for curries or made into oil. It makes soap and margarine.

In south India the coconut is called Green Gold. During the Second World War, soldiers who needed transfusions were given ones of coconut water, being considered sterile.

11

WOOD APPLE TREE

Latin Name	*Aegle marmelos*
English Names	*Wood Apple, Bengal Quince,* *Golden Apple*
Indian Names	*Bengali : Bel* *Gujarati : Bili* *Hindi : Bael, Bilva, Sriphal* *Marathi : Bael* *Sanskrit : Shriphala, Bilva* *Tamil : Vilvum* *Telugu : Muredu*
Family	*Rutaceae*

Aegle is the Latin name for one of the Hesperides, the three sisters who, helped by a dragon, guarded the golden apples of the goddess Hera. *Marmelos* comes from the Portuguese word Marmelosde meaning marbled. The Sanskrit word Shriphala means sacred fruit.

The Bael is considered sacred to Shiva and, as an offering of its leaves is a compulsory ritual, it is usually planted near a Shiva temple. Bilvadandin, he who has a staff of Bilva wood, is another name for Shiva

On the seventh day of Dashehra, the night of the Great Worship, the Rajput kings performed the 'Invitation to the Bael tree', considered the most sacred of Dashehra rites. A Bael fruit was picked fresh from the tree and offered to the fierce goddess Chamunda in order to invoke her protection.

In Bengal, the goddess Durga is aroused from her sleep during Durga Puja by touching a twig from a Bael tree growing in a north-easterly direction. The goddess is invoked to awake and take up her abode in it.

In Bihari folklore common proverbs centre round the tree.

Phir mundlo Bel tar (The bald head will not venture under the Bael tree again). The Bael fruit is said to be attracted to shaven heads and will never resist a chance to fall on one. The English equivalent would be 'once bitten twice shy'.

A proverb illustrating indifference says, '*Bel pakal, kaua ke baap la ka* (What difference does it make to the crow if the Bel fruit is ripe). The crow, which pecks at all ripe fruit, cannot penetrate the hard shell of the Bel, so it is immaterial to the bird when the fruit ripens.

It is said that the presence of a Bael and a Ber tree together indicates an underground spring.

According to Tantric folklore, Lakshmi came down to Earth in the form of a cow. From the dung of this sacred animal arose the Bilva tree. Lakshmi, depicted in the Bhuvaneshvari Tantra, holds a Bilva fruit in her lower left hand, an image that signifies her as the deliverer of the fruits of one's actions.

People go round the Bael tree before starting something, as the tree is supposed to grant success in new ventures. Vasuman, the king of the Videhas, is said to have regained his lost kingdom by going round the Bael tree at the temple of Tiruvidaimarudur.

Lakshmi's sacrifice
(Brihatdharma Purana)

Goddess Lakshmi was the consort of the god Vishnu. And because each god had his own place and impor-

tance she worshipped the god Shiva. Every day
Lakshmi had a thousand lotus flowers plucked by her
handmaidens and she offered them to the idol of Shiva
in the evening. One day, counting the flowers as she
offered them, she found that there were two less than
a thousand. It was too late to pluck any more for
evening had come and the lotuses had closed their
petals for the night.

Lakshmi thought it inauspicious to offer less than a
thousand. Suddenly she remembered that Vishnu had
once described her breasts as blooming lotuses. She
decided to offer them as the two missing flowers.

Lakshmi cut off one breast and placed it with the
flowers on the altar. Before she could cut off the other,
Shiva, who was extremely moved by her devotion,
appeared before her and asked her to stop.

He turned her cut breast into round, sacred Bael
fruit and sent it to Earth to flourish near his temples.

The two friends
(Skanda Purana)

In the beginning of Creation, Brahma the Creator
made things for man and the Earth. One of them was
the Bilva tree. A man sat under this tree and began to
worship the god Vishnu. Brahma named him Bilva.
Pleased with his piety and devotion, Indra, the king of
the gods, asked Bilva to turn the wheel of administration of the Earth. (This was before kings and queens.)

"I will accept the responsibility", said Bilva, "only
if you give me your diamond weapon so that I can
punish wrongdoers".

Indra told Bilva that the weapon would appear when
he desired it.

Bilva built his house under the Bilva tree and ran the Earth.

Kapila, a worshipper of Shiva, came to Bilva's house and they became good friends. One day both of them got into an argument about whether it was better to do penance, as the worshippers of Vishnu did, or do one's duty in the world as Shiva's followers did. Bilva's temper rose during the debate and, summoning the diamond weapon, he cut off Kapila's head.

Now Kapila was immortal, but Bilva didn't know that. This deed was the turning point. He stopped the administration of the Earth. Full of remorse he left the Bilva tree and went to the forest of Mahakala where he became a devotee of Shiva.

Many centuries later Kapila came by that way. He chanced upon Bilva who greeted his friend with amazement and then great honour and love. The two became fast friends again.

Why Brahmins remain poor

The Bael tree is supposed to be the abode of Lakshmi, the goddess of fortune and consort of Vishnu. In fact, Bilvapatrika, she who lives in the leaves of the Bilva tree, is another name for Lakshmi.

Lakshmi enters mortal homes and those whom she blesses prosper and are happy. But Lakshmi is supposed never to have entered a Brahmin's house.

"Why?" asked Vishnu of his consort. "Brahmins keep the temples. They are holy and pious and worship all of us. Why are you so adamant about not blessing them with your luck?"

Lakshmi answered petulantly, "All Brahmins are my natural enemies. I cannot even rest peacefully in my house, the Bael tree, for every day they pluck leaves of it and offer them to Shankara (Shiva). If they destroy my house why should I enter theirs?"

And Vishnu had no answer to this.

The hunter's worship
(Kathasaritsagara)

This hunter lived in Varanasi. He was not religious, in fact, he did not believe in going to temples or in observing any rituals to please the gods.

One day he went hunting in the forest. He chased a deer deep into the forest but he could not kill it. By the time he gave up the chase it was night and the hunter was too tired to find his way back. So he climbed a Bael tree and started breaking the leaves to make a soft perch so that he could spend the night comfortably.

A small Shiva temple had been made at the base of the tree trunk and as the hunter plucked the leaves, a few of them fell on the Shivalinga. The hunter perspired from his efforts and a drop of his sweat fell on the Shivalinga too. He had not eaten at all that day for he had been hunting game since dawn. So you could say the hunter had been fasting. And the day was the fourteenth day on the dark phase of the moon in the month of Phalguna (mid-February to mid-March), a day sacred to Shiva.

The hunter had, without knowing, fulfilled all the conditions for the worship of Shiva. This pleased the god so much that when the hunter died he went, in spite of being an unbeliever, straight to heaven.

The Bael tree is medium-sized and deciduous. It has a rough grey bark and its light brown branches have straight one-inch thorns on them.

74

The leaves are trifoliate and alternate. Each leaf has translucent dots on it. The leaflets are oblong in shape. The greenish-white flowers are sweet-scented.

The fruit is large and round. It has a greenish grey woody shell. The orange pulp inside has many seeds covered with fibrous hair.

The Bael fruit pulp is made into sherbet. It is used as a specific cure for dysentery, mixed with lime to make cement and used in paints for a glossy finish. The wood is used for houses, carts and tool handles. The unripe rind makes a yellow dye used in calico printing. The leaves make poultices for the eyes and the roots are used for the treatment of fever.

12

TEAK TREE

Latin Name	*Tectona grandis*
English Names	*Teak Tree, Indian Oak*
Indian Names	*Bengali : Segun*
	Gujarati : Saga
	Hindi : Sagun, Saigun
	Marathi : Sagvan
	Sanskrit : Shaka
	Tamil : Tekkumaram
	Telugu : Teeku
Family	Verbenaceae

The words *Tectona* and teak come from the Malayalam Tekka which first went into the Portuguese language as Teca. It means carpenter. *Grandis* means large. The Sanskrit word Shaka means, curiously enough, power, strength, and vegetable.

According to Hindu mythology, when the world was divided into Dvipas or islands surrounded by the Sea of Milk, one of them was named Shaka after the Teak tree that grew there.

The girl whose lover was a tree
(Chongli tribal legend from Nagaland)

Once upon a time there was a rich man who had a beautiful daughter. Many men wanted to marry her but she refused them all.

The girl lived in a dormitory with all the other marriageable girls of the village. Her heart had been given to a youth who used to come to her secretly every night in the dormitory and leave at dawn.

During the day, the girl hunted for her lover in the village but she could never find him. At last she told her parents about him.

The father was determined to find out who his daughter's lover was. So, one night, he hid himself outside the dormitory and kept watch.

The youth entered the dormitory silently. At dawn he came out. The father followed. Instead of going to his own dormitory or gorung, the youth headed outside the gate of the village and towards the spring. As soon as he reached the water a strange transformation took place. His arms turned into branches, his hair into leaves and his earrings into white clusters of flowers. Soon instead of a man there was a tall tree.

The father was determined to cut down this magic tree so that his daughter could marry a normal human. When it was fully light he called all his friends and relatives to help him. They cut and cut but the tree would not fall. At last it came down with a crash. In the moment of its death, one wood chip flew far. It reached the girl, pierced her through the eye and went right through to her brain.

The father, rejoicing at the destruction of the tree, came back to his hut only to find that the two lovers had died together.

The prince and the peacock fans

Once upon a time there lived a rich merchant who had seven daughters. He was very arrogant about his wealth and lost no opportunity to show it off. One day, lacking an audience, he called his seven daughters and asked them, "Whose fortune keeps you alive and happy?" Six daughters replied, "Yours, Papa." But the youngest was wilful and she said, "I am alive and happy because of my own good fortune".

"Very well", said her angered father. "Let me see how far your good fortune carries you, Miss." He called his palanquin bearers and sent her away to the dense forest. He allowed her to take only her box of sewing needles and thread and an old nurse who had been with her since she was born.

The two women were set down at sunset at the foot of a large Teak tree. The palanquin bearers saluted them and were gone.

The gigantic Teak tree looked down at the little fourteen-year-old crying with fear. "Unhappy girl", it said, "soon the wild beasts of the jungle will come out and eat you up."

But as it spoke, the girl looked so piteous that its heart softened. "All right, don't cry. I will help you. I will open my trunk and both of you can hide in it."

The Teak split its trunk and the girl and her nurse climbed into the hollow. The tree closed back into its natural shape.

The wild beasts came out at night. Prowling round the jungle, they smelt humans. "We know you are hiding humans within you", they howled at the Teak tree. They dashed against the tree, clawed its bark into shreds, broke its branches and scattered its leaves. But the tree would not surrender the fugitives, even though blood ran from its pierced bark.

As dawn broke, the wild beasts returned to their lairs. The exhausted tree split open and the two women came out. They saw the gaping wounds of the tree.

"Good tree", said the girl and embraced it. "You have given us shelter at a heavy cost. We are grateful." She went to the banks of a nearby river and brought back fistfuls of mud which she smeared on the open gashes of the trunk.

The tree felt better. "But you must be hungry", it said to the girl." She nodded.

"Give your nurse whatever money you have and let her go to the city and buy some khai (roasted rice). The girl took out a few needles and some golden thread from her sewing box and gave them to her nurse to sell in the city.

The nurse came back with a small sackful of khai. "Eat only half of this", commanded the Teak tree. "Strew the rest on the bank of the river."

The women did as they were told, even though they did not understand why, and then they climbed back inside the tree trunk to sleep.

Flocks of peacocks always came to the river at night. When the birds saw the khai they went mad with delight and struggled and pushed one another to peck each delicious piece of rice off the ground. In this jostle, many of their tail feathers fell off.

When morning came and the women emerged from the trunk, the tree told them, "Go to the riverbed and gather the peacock plumes that you see lying there. Stitch these plumes together into a fan for the king of the city."

The girl sewed the plumes together and the nurse took the fan to the city palace. The king's son saw the fan, liked it and immediately bought it. "Did you make it?" he asked the nurse. "No," she answered, "my little mistress is extremely skilful with her needle and she made it."

With the money the prince had given her, the nurse bought some more khai and again half of it was eaten and half strewn on the bank of the river. Every night the peacocks came and every morning the little girl had enough feathers for a fan. The nurse took the fans to the palace, where they had become very popular with the prince's friends, and sold them to the court.

Every time she met the prince he questioned her about her mistress. "Won't she come to sell them herself?" he asked. "Oh no, Sir", answered the shocked nurse, "my mistress is extremely well born. She would never come to the market."

With the money that the fans brought, the girl made a little house near the Teak tree. She lived there with her nurse. But the prince grew more and more curious about the dextrous seamstress and one day he followed the nurse back from the city and saw the girl. She had grown slender and beautiful. He decided to marry her.

The king and his court came to the forest, for the girl refused to be married anywhere else. The ceremony was held before the Teak tree which was decorated with garlands for the occasion. The bride and groom poured milk at its roots. The merchant and his daughters came for the wedding too. And all thanked the Teak tree for its wisdom and care.

This is a very tall, deciduous tree with a grey brown trunk. The branches are quadrangular and hairy. The large, rough leaves are elliptical in shape, hairless above but covered with dense red hair underneath. They grow in pairs

The flowers emerge in dense white pyramidal clusters at the ends of branches. The fruit is round, brownish and spongy.

The wood of the teak tree is extremely valuable as it is insect and white ant-proof. It is used for building houses, ships, railway carriages, furniture and musical instruments. The tree also yields a tar oil used as a varnish. From the bark and flowers comes a medicine for bronchitis.

The largest and oldest Teak tree in Asia, supposed to be more than 600 hundred years old, is in Kerala's Parambikulam game sanctuary.

13

ASHOKA TREE

Latin Name	*Saraca indica*
English Name	*Ashoka Tree*
Indian Names	*Bengali : Ashok*
	Hindi : Ashok, Sita Ashok
	Sanskrit : Ashoka, Vanjuladruma,
	* Pallavadru*
	Tamil : Asogam
	Telugu : Asokamu
Family	Caesalpiniaceae

Another name for the tree is *Jonesia asoka* after the
botanist Sir William Jones. The origin of the word
Saraca is obscure. It probably comes from Sarac which
is a genus of small trees whose young leaves hang as
pendulous tassels. *Indica* means of Indian origin. The
Sanskrit word Ashoka means that which is without
grief or that which gives no grief. Pallavadru means the
tree of love blossoms.

The Ashoka is one of the sacred trees for both
Hindus and Buddhists. The day for its worship is the
thirteenth day of the Chaitra month (usually 27 April).
Its beautiful, delicately perfumed flowers are used in
temple decoration.

The tree is a symbol of love and is dedicated to Kama
who uses its blossoms as one of the five arrows in his
quiver. A popular spring festival of olden times was
Asoka Pushpaprachayika, the gathering of Ashoka
flowers. Young women wore all their finery and Ashoka
flowers in their hair. In Bengal the Ashoka Sasthi or

the Griefless Sixth festival is held on the sixth day of the bright fortnight of the month of Baisakh (April-May) when women eat the Ashoka flowerbuds. Drinking the water in which the flowers have been washed is considered a protection against grief. The Ashoka tree is supposed to flower when its roots are pressed by the feet of a beautiful young girl. Women were supposed to dance round the trees and gently touch them with their left foot. According to Sanskrit poetry the Ashoka represents nature which is so sensitive that it bursts into bloom at the touch of a woman.

Kalidasa described the Ashoka tree in *Ritusamhara* as having drooping tassels of silk covered with coral red blossoms which emerged in the springtime and made the hearts of young women burn with desire.

The Ashoka tree is also regarded as a guardian of female chastity. This belief comes from the *Ramayana*. Sita, abducted by the demon Ravana, sat in a grove of Ashoka trees and remained chaste all through the long years that she was forced to stay in Lanka.

The tree was very popular with the Mathura school of sculpture. It is depicted surrounded by female figures who are not dancing girls but Vrikshadevatas or gods of the trees who represented fertility and were worshipped by childless women.

Ashoka trees are always planted in Buddhist monasteries. In the legend of Buddha, when Maya, his mother, became aware that she had conceived him she retired to a grove of Ashoka trees. Gautama Buddha was born under one of these trees in the Lumbini garden. Hiuen Tsang, the Chinese traveller who came to India in A.D. 630, mentions seeing the Ashoka tree under which the birth took place. In fact a sapling of the tree was taken by Prince Mahendra, the son of

Emperor Ashoka, to Ceylon in about 250 B.C. and was planted in Anuradhapur. Its great branches are now supported by pillars and it is the oldest tree of historical importance in the world.

The cannibal's reformation
(Bhavishya Purana)

Sashoka was a Bhil cannibal. He hid in the forest and ambushed travellers who passed through it. He would cut them up, roast them and eat them.

One day, while on the prowl, he saw a small hut on the far side of the forest. He went closer and saw a sage meditating outside it. Sashoka planned to kill him eventually but, since he had never seen a holy man before, he decided to watch him for a while.

The Rishi was in a deep trance, his eyes shut, his face serene. Watching him, Sashoka felt a sudden change of heart. "I wish I could be like that", he thought. "Instead I am hated and feared and shunned by all men."

He went to the sage and knelt before him. The Rishi opened his eyes. "What do you want, my son?" he asked gently. "I already know that you have repented your evil ways. So ask me for any wish and I will grant it."

Sashoka the Bhil said, "Holy sage, I am sick of being evil. Please free me from this life of blood and sin and make me pure again. "

"I do not have the power to grant you this wish", said the Rishi, "in your present life. You must live out the rest of this life in prayer and penance. But do not despair. Vishnu is to be born on this earth as Rama. In that age you will be reborn as a tree in demon Ravana's garden. Sita, the wife of Rama, will be abducted by

Ravana. She will seek refuge under your shade. One day Hanuman, the divine monkey, will sit on you while he consoles the grief-stricken Sita. On that day her grief will disappear and all your previous sins will be washed away. You will be known all the world over as the tree that takes away grief."

And that is how the Ashoka tree came to be.

It is a small to medium sized evergreen tree with an erect trunk. The bark is dark brown, sometimes tending towards black.

The leaves grow alternately on the branches. Each leaf is about a foot long and is divided into four to six pairs of leaflets attached to a smooth round midrib. The leaflets are firm and glossy with wavy margins. The young leaves are copper red, thin and flaccid and hang vertically downwards even after they mature and become deep green.

The fragrant flowers appear in large, compact clusters which spring directly from the branches. On opening the flowers are a bright orange-yellow which later turns to red. Each flower has 4-7 spreading thread-like stamens with kidney-shaped anthers.

The long, flat fruit pod is a fleshy red when unripe and leathery when it matures. It contains smooth grey seeds.

The timber of the Ashoka is used for house-building. Its bark and flowers are used in Ayurvedic medicine.

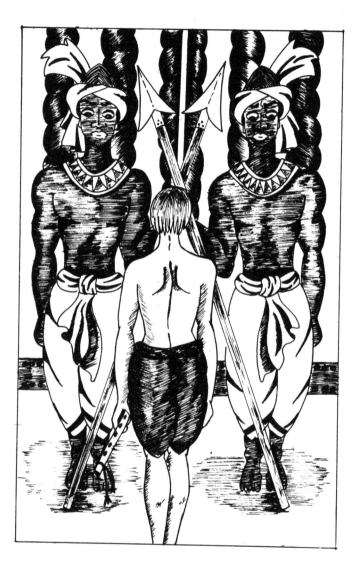

14

DEVIL'S TREE

Latin Name	*Alstonia scholaris*
English Name	*Devil's Tree*
Indian Names	*Bengali : Chhatim*
	Hindi : Chatian
	Kannada : Maddale
	Malayalam : Pala
	Marathi : Satvin, Shaitan
	Sanskrit : Saptaparni
	Tamil : Pala
Family	Apocynaceae

The name *Alstonia* has been given to commemorate Professor C. Alston (1685-1760) of Edinburgh. *Scholaris* refers to the fact that the tree was used earlier for making wooden slates for school children. Both the Sanskrit and the Marathi names Saptaparna and Satvin mean seven-leaved. Shaitan and the English name Devil's Tree refer to the malefic magic properties that folklore endows the tree with.

The tree is protected by its evil reputation. Tribals of the Western Ghats are unwilling to even pass under this tree for fear of its resident evil spirits. To fall asleep under it is considered a certain way to invite death from the tree's guardians.

The shepherd and the spirit
(Folk tale from Madhya Pradesh)

Once upon a time, in the Western Ghats or hills of India lived a shepherd called Ramu who played the flute beautifully. Every day while his goats grazed in the mountains, Ramu sat under the Chatian tree and played his flute.

Now, in this Chatian tree lived a fierce spirit. When Ramu first came to sit under the tree he was just about to strike him dead when he heard the boy's flute and was charmed by the melody.

The spirit danced among the leaves and branches. Soon, when he was used to Ramu coming every day, he ventured down from the tree and introduced himself. From then on Ramu would play and the spirit would dance in great happiness. The two became good friends.

One day, the king's son happened to be passing by and he heard Ramu's music. He stopped, bewitched by the lilting notes. He approached the shepherd boy who stopped on seeing the richly clad stranger. "Play for me every day", said the prince, "and you shall be my friend. When I become king I shall make you a minister of this land." Ramu was delighted and played a merry tune on his flute in response.

As soon as the prince rode away, the spirit came down from the tree where he had sat glowering all this while. "Don't believe this man. He is rich and rich men forget their friends soon." But Ramu was simple and dazzled by the prince's splendour. He refused to believe the spirit.

The prince came every day and Ramu neglected his goats while he played for him. The spirit felt very left out. He sulked and refused to come down from the Chatian tree any more.

A few months later the king of the land died. It was announced that the royal prince would be crowned. Ramu was so excited.

"I shall go and congratulate my friend", he said to the spirit. He put on his best clothes and set out for the city. He reached the palace gates but the guards refused to let him inside.

"The king is my friend", protested Ramu, "he will want to see me. "

"Of course", mocked the guards. "Every beggar who comes this way is a personal friend of His Majesty." They pushed him away.

Just then the royal gates opened and the king's carriage emerged. Ramu called out, "My friend, my friend, I am Ramu the flute boy, Ramu the shepherd. These guards are not letting me in to see you. "

But the king was blinded by his own importance and did not or seemed not to recognize the humble peasant boy. "He must be mad", he informed the guards. "See that he is driven away. "And his carriage passed on.

The guards set upon Ramu and taunting and jeering they drove him away from the palace gates. The shepherd boy was broken-hearted. He walked back many miles, dusty and sore, and sat dejected under the Chatian tree.

He was silent for many hours. The spirit watched the tears trickle down his face. At first he did not want to say anything, for he was still sulking. But the misery of the boy was too much to bear and he came down from the tree.

"Where is your flute, boy?" he asked sarcastically. "Why are you quiet? Let us make merry now that you are to be a minister."

Ramu burst out crying. He told his tale of woe to the spirit. "You were right all along", he admitted. "I am only a poor shepherd. How can the king be friends with me. "

The spirit was furious. He flew with the wind to the palace of the king. "I will punish this arrogant king for having made my Ramu so unhappy." He cast a spell on the king and suddenly, in full view of the court, the king sprouted horns and long, long front teeth.

The king and the court were horrified. In the days that followed doctors from all over the kingdom were summoned; sorcerers and wise men flocked to the court. But no one could cure the king. Word of the king's state spread throughout the kingdom.

Ramu was a kind-hearted boy. When he heard of the king's misfortune, he felt very sorry for him. But the spirit was delighted. "I did it", he bragged. "He caused you so much unhappiness. Let him be unhappy too."

But Ramu begged the spirit to relent. When the spirit did not give in, Ramu threatened to stop playing his flute.

"All right, all right", said the spirit of the Chatian Tree sulkily. "Here, take a branch of this Chatian and wave it thrice round the king. And say, the spirits of the Chatian Tree release you from their magic."

This time Ramu was let into the palace, for the king had left instructions that anyone who promised a cure for his monstrous state should be brought in without delay. He walked up to the throne where the king sat huddled in shame. He waved the Chatian branch and said the magic words. Immediately the king was restored his former face.

The court gave a gasp. The king recognized Ramu now and hugged the flute boy. "I am sorry I did not recognize you that day", he said. "But you are truly my friend. Come and be a minister and stay in my palace."

But Ramu had learnt his lesson. He thanked the king and refused the honour. "I am only a shepherd", he said. "All I know is how to play the flute."

Ramu came back to the Chatian Tree. Every day he played his flute and the spirit danced in joy every day and both of them spent their lives in peace and happiness.

It is a tall evergreen tree with a rough greyish bark. The branches are whorled, that is, several of them come out of the main trunk at the same height like the ribs of an umbrella.

The leaves are leathery and oblong, tapering to a lance-shape. They are dark green above and whitish underneath. Seven of them come out together in round whorls.

The scented, greenish white flower-clusters bloom on long stalks at the end of the branches. The fruit is long, narrow and hangs in pairs, forming dense clusters.

The wood is soft and is used for making packing cases, matchsticks and pencils.

15

BLACK PLUM

Latin Names	*Eugenia jambolana* *Syzygium cumini*
English Names	*Java Plum, Black Plum, Indian Blackberry, Indian Allspice*
Indian Names	*Bengali : Kalojam, Jam* *Hindi : Jamun, Phalinda* *Marathi : Jambhul* *Sanskrit : Jambu, Phalendra* *Tamil : Naval, Nagai* *Telugu : Neredu*
Family	Myrtaceae

Eugenia comes from Eugene, Prince of Savoy, a patron of botany in the seventeenth century. *Syzygium* is from the Greek Suzogos or paired. *Jambolana* comes from the East Indies word Jambos or Rose Apple which found its way into Hindi as Jambu and then Jamun. Phalendra means chief of fruit-giving plants.

The Jamun tree is considered sacred to both Krishna and Ganesha. It is venerated by Buddhists too. The god of the clouds, Megha, is supposed to have been incarnated on the earth as the Jamun and that is why the colour of the fruit is that of the sky when a storm approaches. The leaves of this tree are strung into garlands and hung over the entrance doors of houses to ensure perpetuity and continuity and a stable marriage. Planted near temples, Brahmins are fed in its shade.

The monkey's heart

On the banks of the Yamuna river grew a Jamun tree. A monkey family made this tree their home. The monkey husband was a friendly fellow. He loved the purple Jamun fruit and ate greedily of it, but he was willing to share it too.

Across the banks of the river lived an alligator family. The male crocodile swam across to the bank of the Jamun tree every day to sun himself. The monkey and the alligator became good friends and the alligator ate Jamuns given to him by the monkey.

One day the monkey, seeing the enjoyment of the alligator when he clamped his jaws on the fruit, said, "Alligator, my friend, why don't you take some fruit home for your wife today. "

"What a good idea", said the alligator. The monkey collected some fruit and when the evening darkness deepened, the alligator swam back to his home.

His wife ate the fruit. Her eyes slit with enjoyment and her jaws yawned with pleasure. "My husband", she said, "where did you get this tender, sweet fruit?" The alligator told her about the monkey that lived on the tree and distributed the fruit.

The alligator's wife grew silent as she thought. Saliva dripped from the corners of her mouth. "If these Jamuns are so sweet," she mused, "how much sweeter would be the heart of one who lives on them."

She ordered her husband, "Bring me the monkey tomorrow. I will eat his heart."

The alligator was horrified. He tried to remonstrate with his wife but she was adamant.

The next day, a tense alligator came to the bank of the Jamun tree. "My wife thanks you for the delicious fruit." His eyes avoided the monkey's as he spoke. "She would like to repay your hospitality by inviting you to dinner."

The monkey did not see anything strange in his friend's behaviour. "Certainly," he said. "Let's go. It will make a change from the Jamun fruit." He sat on the alligator's back and the latter pushed himself sluggishly into the water.

The journey was a silent one. Half-way through the monkey looked down and saw the alligator crying, tears streaming out to join the water of the river. "What is it, my friend, what makes you so sad?" he asked concernedly.

The alligator replied, "Forgive me, monkey. I have tricked you. My wife is not going to feed you. She desires to eat your heart for she says that it must be as sweet as the Jamun fruit you eat. And I am too scared of her not to bring you. Forgive me."

The monkey gave a little jump of alarm. First he thought that he would plead with the alligator but saw that that would be of no use. So he thought quickly and said, "Oh my, is that all? There is no need to be unhappy, alligator. I will happily give my heart to your wife. What need have monkeys for hearts?"

"But", he continued blithely, "unfortunately today is the day that I wash my heart. Early this morning I soaked it in the river and hung it out to dry on the branches of the Jamun tree. Let us go back and collect it."

Alligators are not known for their intelligence. And this one's grief clouded his commonsense even more. "Very well", said the alligator, relieved that his friend had taken the news so well. He turned around and the pair headed back to the banks of the tree. As soon as they neared the tree, before the alligator could see that there was no heart drying on its limbs, the monkey leapt and caught a branch.

From that day on, the monkey refused to come down from the Jamun tree. But, because he was a generous soul, he threw the fruit down to the alligator who sunned himself on the banks of the river.

It is a large, dense, long-lived, evergreen tree. Its bark is light grey with patches of dark grey.

The leaves are smooth and oval, growing in pairs. When turned to the sun, each leaf is shown to have pellucid, translucent dots on it. When the leaves are crushed they have a strong smell, almost like turpentine.

The flowers are small and a dirty white green. They are faintly scented and grow in large bunches massed on stalks that come out below the leaves. The petals remain stuck together instead of opening out and fall off in one piece.

The fruit is a small juicy oval, plum pink and green at first then turning purple black as it ripens. Each fruit contains one large seed.

The leaves of the Jamun tree are fed to Tasar silkworms. The fruit is juicy and sweet and is eaten by people, birds and even horses. It is also turned into juice, vinegar and alcohol. The seed is used in medicines for diabetes and also fed to cattle. The timber makes agricultural implements.

16

MANGO

Latin Name	*Mangifera indica*
English Name	*Mango*
Indian Names	*Gujarati : Amri*
	Hindi : Aam
	Malayalam : Amram, Mahu
	Marathi : Amha
	Punjabi : Amb
	Sanskrit : Amra
	Tamil : Mangas
	Telugu : Mamada
Family	*Anacardiaceae*

The word Mango probably comes from the Tamil word Mangas or the Malayan word Mangga or the Portuguese word Manga. *Mangifera indica* means the Indian mango-bearing tree. The Sanskrit word for mango, Amra, also means a particular weight.

The mango tree has been cultivated in India for more than 4000 years. It was found by Alexander's army when it entered the Indus Valley in 327 BC. Representations of it are found on the Stupa of Barhut and Sanchi dated 150 BC.

It is symbolized in Hindu mythology as a wish-granting tree and a symbol of love and devotion. Kalidasa mentions it as one of the arrows of Kama, the god of love. It is supposed to be an incarnation of Prajapati, the Lord of all creatures. Its flowers are dedicated to the moon.

Other legends say that it was brought from Lanka to India by Hanuman. Hanuman, taking a message from Rama to Sita, leapt from tree to tree. Resting for a while on the Mango tree, he was so delighted with the flavour of its fruit that he threw the seeds into the sea and they floated across to India and took root.

It is believed that Shiva married Parvati under a Mango tree. So marriage pandals are festooned with strings of Mango leaves. The wood is used in funeral pyres. Village superstition has it that at every birth, the mango tree sprouts new leaves and so Mango leaf garlands are hung over the door of the house where a son has been born.

Spirits of dead ancestors are supposed to live in this tree. Baji Rao's ancestors had murdered the Maratha Peshwa Narayan Rao in 1772 and taken his throne. Baji Rao believed himself to be haunted by the spirit of Narayan Rao. He ordered several thousand Mango trees planted around Poona to give shelter to the angry spirit.

In aboriginal India, the bride and bridegroom walk several times round the Mango tree before the actual ceremony of marriage takes place. The groom smears the Mango bark with vermilion and embraces it. The bride does the same thing to the Mahua tree. Tribal songs and riddles usually centre round flora and fauna and the Mango tree has its share. From Chhatisgarh comes this riddle:

Nilai beti, jhula bathi
Lai re saga thai beti."

The young daughter sits on a swing.
Oh kinsman, I warn you to keep a watch on her.

(The green mango which must be protected from birds and human marauders)

An Oriya song of the Dewar tribe highlights the sacredness or the love in which the tribals hold the tree.

> You have cut a Banyan
> You have cut a Pipal
> But why did you cut the Mango tree?
> It was as if you were carrying
> A cow's leg upon your head.
> Why have you cast away your virtue?
> Why have you killed your nephew?

How do the villagers of Uttar Pradesh make the Mango tree give fruit?

If the tree shows no sign of fruiting, the owner of the tree collects a few of his friends and arming himself with an axe, he walks up to the tree.

"What is all this?" he says in a threatening tone. "No fruit. Do you think you will make a fool of me. I will soon show you who is the fool." As he says this he hits the trunk of the tree with his axe.

As soon as he hits the tree, his friends fling themselves upon him and seize his hands. "We implore you, do not be so harsh. Spare this poor tree and it will behave itself in future", they plead.

"Do you guarantee this wretched tree's behavior?" asks the owner loudly.

"Yes, yes", the friends reply.

"I don't believe you." The owner wrenches himself free and gives the tree another blow with his axe.

The friends place themselves between him and the tree. They beg him to spare the tree. After a great deal of persuasion the owner agrees and strides away without a backward glance.

The friends turn to the tree and say, "Brother tree, we have saved you this time, or your owner would have chopped you down. Now you had better bear plenty of fruit next year to show him that you are on your best behaviour. Otherwise we will not be able to help you next time."

It is said that this method never fails.

Buddha and the monkeys
(Mahakapi Jataka)

Once upon a time the Buddha was born as Mahakapi, the king of the monkeys. He and his eighty thousand monkeys lived on a single Mango tree in the middle of a thick forest on the banks of the Ganges river.

Mahakapi told his tribe not to let a single Mango fall on the ground. "If man tastes this fruit", he said, "he will want it all and he will destroy us for it."

One day, quite by chance, a Mango escaped the attention of the monkeys. It fell into the river and was carried downstream.

Brahmadatta, King of Kashi, was bathing in the river. He saw the strange fruit in the water and, reaching out, he seized it. He smelt its freshness and squeezing it put a bit of the juice in his mouth.

He was enchanted by its sweetness. "I must have the tree that grows this fruit", he said. He ordered his courtiers to row upstream in boats till they found the tree, and he ordered his army to follow the course of the river.

Many days later, the men came to the Mango tree, its branches laden with fruit. King Brahmadatta saw the monkeys. "Surround the forest" he ordered."Kill all the monkeys, otherwise they will eat my fruit."

The monkeys went trembling with fright to Mahakapi. "Save us, Lord", they begged.

Mahakapi climbed a branch that stretched to the other bank of the Ganges and, springing from, it, he jumped to the other side. He cut a bamboo and fastened it to the branch to make a bridge that all the monkeys could climb over to escape. But the bamboo was short so he stretched out his body to complete the bridge.

The monkeys climbed over the body of their lord and escaped to the other bank of the river and away from the army. But one monkey, Devadatta, the cousin of Buddha, who had also been born in that incarnation, hated him. When his turn came to cross, he stamped so heavily on Mahakapi's back that it broke.

Mahakapi was alone and in great pain. King Brahmadatta who had been watching the great escape and who felt nothing but admiration for the monkey king, had him brought down from the tree.

Mahakapi was received with honour. He was washed and oiled and his body clothed. He instructed the king on his duties to the lowest of his subjects and then, his body wracked with pain, he died. King Brahmadatta put a shrine at the foot of the Mango tree to honour the memory of Mahakapi, the king of the monkeys.

The princess who became a mango tree

The daughter of Surya, the Sun god, was the wife of a handsome king. One day while she was walking in a nearby forest she was chased by a Rakshasi, or demoness. She fled through the forest but the Rakshasi drew closer and closer. To escape her pursuer, the girl changed herself into a lotus in the forest pool.

The Rakshasi could not enter the pool. So she kept guard over it instead. The king returned to find his wife missing and, as he loved her dearly, he got on his horse and set off to find her. One day he was passing through the forest and he saw this single beautiful flower growing in the stillness of the pool. He wanted to take it with him to his palace. He waded into the water and plucked it.

The Rakshasi was angered. A single blazing look from her eye and the flower was burnt. The king was alarmed and he threw the ashes by the side of the lake and rode away. The Rakshasi also went away satisfied that she had destroyed the girl.

From the ashes of the lotus flower grew the Mango tree. A few years later the king, passing through the forest still in search of his wife, saw the ripe fruit and took it back with him to the palace as a novelty to show the courtiers.

But as he passed it to his minister the fruit fell on the ground. From it emerged the daughter of the Sun God, the wife of the king. The royal pair were united and lived happily ever after.

It is a large, evergreen tree with a densely rounded crown. The bark is thick, rough and flaking.

The leaves are stiff, narrow, glossy and leathery and grow alternately. They are lance-shaped, tapering at both ends with wavy edges. When crushed, they have a strong smell.

The flowers are small. The petals are pale yellow-green with a touch of pink-purple at the base. They grow in pyramidal bunches at the ends of stalks.

The fruit is kidney-shaped, fleshy and fibrous, with a dark stone in the middle. The unripe fruit is dark green, gradually turning yellow, orange or red according to the variety. It has a tough, thin skin.

The Mango tree is used mainly for its fruit which is rich in vitamins. Preserves and pickles are made from the unripe fruit and its pulp is dried and used as a curry base. The wood is used for packing cases. The gum of the bark, the seeds which contain gallic acid and the astringent leaves, are all three used in medicines.

The largest Mango tree in the world grows in a village called Burail in Ambala. It has been given the name of Chhappar or roof thatch probably because it gives shade to so many. The area covered by the crown is 2,700 yards and its average yearly yield of fruit is reported to be 450 maunds, or around 175 quintals.

17

KADAMBA

Latin Name	*Adina cordifolia*
English Name	*Anthocephelus kadamba*
Indian names	*Bengali : Kadamba, Kadam*
	Hindi : Kadam, Kadamba
	Malayalam : Attutek
	Marathi : Heddi
	Oriya : Karam
	Sanskrit : Kadamba, Neepa
	Tamil : Kadamba, Manja
	Telugu : Kadambamu,
	Pasupukadamba
Family	Rubiaceae

Adina comes from the Greek word Adinos meaning crowded. This refers to the crowding of the flowers in dense balls. *Cordifolia* means with heart-shaped leaves. In Sanskrit, Neepa means deep rooted.

The Kadamba tree is associated in Sanskrit literature with the monsoons. It is said to bloom only when it hears the roar of thunderclouds. The breeze that accompanies the rains is called Kadambanila or with the fragrance of the Kadamba. The rainwater that collects in the hollow places of the tree when it is in full bloom is called Kadambara and is said to be imbued with honey.

The Kadamba is associated with Krishna who is usually shown playing his flute under it. It is believed that when Kaliya Naga, the giant snake whose breath was so venomous that all creatures that came within a

few miles of it were destroyed, inhabited the Kaliyada-ha lake (before he was killed by Krishna) and the only thing that grew on a small island in the middle of the lake was the Kadamba tree. And it was immortal because Garuda, the eagle, had perched on it when he flew back from Svargaloka after drinking amrita, the drink which immortalizes. As he sat on a branch of the Kadamba, he wiped his beak against its branches and a drop of amrita fell on the tree and made it immortal.

Another superstition has to do with the founding of the city of Madras. The god Indra killed the asura or demon Vrinda. He was cursed for Brahmahatya, the slaying of a Brahmin. To shake off the curse he was told to find the most sacred spot on earth. Indra wandered all over and in his travels he passed through a forest of Kadamba trees. Suddenly the curse lifted from him and he became free. He looked around him to see where the sacred spot could be. He saw the god Shiva in the form of a Lingam, reclining under the shade of a beautiful Kadamba tree. Indra built a huge canopy over this Lingam and the first modern temple came into being. The forest became in time the city of Madras.

The Kadam festival in Orissa and West Bengal is celebrated by agricultural communities. On the eleventh day of the bright fortnight of Bhadra, the Kadam tree is planted ceremoniously. Leaves of the Sal tree are offered to it along with cucumber and vermilion. This is followed by music and dance. The worship of the Kadam tree is supposed to ensure wealth and children.

The trader's children

(Folk tale from Orissa)

Once upon a time lived a rich trader who had seven daughters and seven sons. All his sons were married, so he had seven daughters-in-law as well.

One day the man had to leave on a long journey. He called his large family together and told them that they must work extremely hard to increase the riches of the family in his absence. He told them that he would not tolerate any laziness and that he expected to find the family fortune doubled on his return.

In his absence his children worked very hard. The daughters and daughters-in-law winnowed grain, cleaned condiments and masalas, wove cloth and sewed clothes while the sons travelled far and wide to the villages selling these wares. But in spite of their hard work their wealth did not increase.

One day a Brahmin passed by and the family invited him in to share their meal. Listening to their woes, the Brahmin said, "My children, only the Karam Raja and the Karam Rani, the spirits of the Karam tree, can bring you wealth. You must worship them."

The children asked the Brahmin to stay in their house while he taught them the rituals of worship. This he did and soon the household made preparations for the festival.

The day of worship dawned and the children went to the Karam tree and built a shrine under it. They offered flowers and sweets and then they linked hands and sang and danced. While they were absorbed in this, the rich trader returned home. He saw his children singing and dancing and jumped to the conclusion that

110

this was all they had been doing since he had gone away.

"I'll teach you to waste time!" he said in a fury. He kicked the shrine down and set upon his children with a stout stick.

The Karam Raja and Karam Rani were deeply offended. They left the village tree and went into the jungle to live in a Kadamba tree that grew there. And with them they took the luck of the village. The village Kadamba tree died.

The trader got poorer and poorer. Sometimes his wares were not good. Sometimes people did not want to buy from him. Sometimes there was illness in the family and the money went in buying medicine. His children sulked. The last straw was a thief running away with the remaining money in the house. The merchant could not understand why this was happening to him.

"It is simple", explained the same Brahmin, passing through the village again. "You have offended Karam Raja and Karam Rani. You must bring them back."

In despair, the trader went to the forest and after bowing to the Kadam tree, cut off a branch and planted it in the courtyard of his house. The branch was worshipped every day and a small shrine made at its base. It grew into a tall tree and luck returned to the trader and his family. From then on the Karam festival is celebrated in Orissa at the beginning of December.

The seventh son's luck

(Legend from the Bhuiya tribe of Keonjhar)

Long ago there was a Bhuiya merchant who had seven sons. Six of them were married and worked very hard. The seventh was considered good for nothing. He did

111

no work, spending all his time worshipping the Karam tree. He would fast all day and dance round the tree beating a drum that he had made of the stalk of a plaintain tree.

The family grew richer and richer. Wealth made the six brothers greedy and angry and they decided not to share any of their money with the youngest. "Why should he too be an heir when he does no work at all?" they said. They broke his drum and drove him out of the house. The boy went away and lived under the Karam tree in the forest.

With the boy's going, the worship of the Karam tree came to an end. The merchant's wealth became less and less and soon the family had no money at all. In despair the merchant sat at his family shrine and said, "Bhagwant, why has this happened to me? I work hard but no result seems to come of it." And the deity answered, "It is because you do not worship the Karam Raja any more. The devotion of your youngest son made your family wealthy. But you threw him out."

The merchant rushed to the forest and begged forgiveness of his youngest son. He was welcomed home and he started the worship of the Karam tree again. The family prospered and the festival is held yearly.

It is a large, deciduous tree with horizontal branches.

The paired leaves are large and shiny, broadly oval and heart-shaped at the base. They are slightly hairy and when young, tinged with pink. They are characterized by very prominent parallel veins.

The flowers are small and golden yellow, clustered together in rounded heads slightly smaller than a golf ball. Their styles form a halo round the ball leading to the description of "a treasure so wondrous, of hairy golden orbs."

The fruit is minute, clustering together to form black balls.

The timber is used for matches and plywood. The bark of the tree is used as an antiseptic.

18

TULIP TREE

Latin Name	*Thespesia populnea*
English Names	*Tulip Tree, Umbrella Tree, Portia Tree*
Indian Names	*Bengali : Dumbla, Paras Pipal, Gajashundi* *Hindi : Bhendi, Parsipu* *Malayalam : Chandamaram, Puvarusu* *Marathi : Bhendi* *Sanskrit : Gandha Bhanda* *Tamil : Kallal, Pursa, Porsung* *Telugu : Gangareni*
Family	Malvaceae

Thespesia means Divine in Greek because Captain Cook, who discovered it in Tahiti, found that it was always planted near temples. *Populnea* means Poplar-like and refers to the shape of the leaves. Umbrella comes from the dense crown which forms an umbrella shape. Its flowers resemble those of the Lady's finger or Okra plant, also called Bhendi, and so it gets its Indian name.

Rooplakshmi's colours

Once upon a time there was a king who had a very beautiful daughter called Rooplakshmi. Unfortunately Rooplakshmi had been told so many times that she was beautiful that she grew very vain. She thought about her beauty all the time.

113

Every morning the princess and her friends went to a nearby temple. One day, as her chariot neared the temple, a holy man was passing by. He hailed the chariot to stop and asked the princess for food.

But Rooplakshmi did not hear him. She was absorbed in admiring her reflection in the polished metal of the chariot sides. She had no idea, as usual, of the outside world.

Insulted and angry, the holy man turned her into a tree.

Rooplakshmi's friends rushed back in panic and informed the king. The king came in his chariot to the temple and fell at the feet of the holy man. "Please, Rishi", he begged, "take back your curse. She is only a thoughtless girl. She meant no harm."

The holy man felt sorry that he had cursed Rooplakshmi but he could not undo it now. "I do not know how to take back my curse", he admitted. "All I can offer is that the flowers of this tree will be of the colours that Rooplakshmi wore this morning, they will be very beautiful and whoever sees them will be enchanted by their loveliness."

And so was born the Bhendi tree and Rooplakshmi's beauty became eternal.

It is a small to medium-sized evergreen tree. Its smooth grey trunk is tall and straight and its branches are close-set.

The leaves are smooth, broad and heart shaped, tapering at the ends like the leaves of a Peepal tree. They grow alternately and both sides have a few tiny ash coloured spots. The leaves turn yellow before falling.

The flowers grow singly or in pairs. They are pale lemon yellow cups with a deep maroon centre. When they wither they turn salmon pink and then a dull purple. Each petal looks crushed and twisted.

The turban-shaped fruit contains five cells, each packed with egg-shaped seeds. The fruit turns from green, when young, to brown and then black.

The timber of the Bhendi tree is used for cart wheels, gunstocks, boats and house building. The bark and heartwood yield tannin and are used for a red dye. The fibre from the inner bark makes ropes and gunny bags. From the flowers and fruit comes a yellow dye and a medicine for skin diseases and migraine. The leaves become food wrappers.

19

INDIAN CORK TREE

Latin name	*Millingtonia hortensis*
English Names	*Indian Cork Tree, Tree Jasmine*
Indian Names	*Bengali : Akash Nim, Cork Gach*
	Hindi : Nim Chameli, Akash Nim
	Malayalam : Katesam
	Tamil : Maramalli, Karkku
	Telugu : Kavuku
Family	Bignoniaceae

Millingtonia is named after Sir Thomas Millington (1628-1704), English professor at Oxford. *Hortensis* means of gardens . From the bark an inferior type of cork is made, giving it its English name.

The wicked sisters-in-law

Chameli was a pretty, young girl. She had six elder brothers, all of whom doted on her. They brought her pretty clothes and gave her the best things to eat. She was given so much love that the wives of the six brothers grew jealous.

One day the brothers had to leave their home on work. Before they left the brothers called their six wives and said, "We are leaving our sister Chameli in your care. See that she is treated with as much affection as she is accustomed to."

The wives promised to do so. But as soon as the brothers left, they sent for Chameli. They took away her fine clothes and made her wear rags.

"From today you will do all the work in the house", they ordered.

Chameli washed the clothes, swept the floors, dusted and cleaned, and cooked. She was not given enough food, only the left-overs. At night she shivered in the cold. Her sisters-in-law beat her regularly.

Chameli had been brought up delicately. She could not bear this ill-treatment for long and soon she fell ill and died.

The sisters-in-law grew frightened. They did not tell anyone of her death for the marks of their beatings showed clearly. They waited until dark and then buried her in a corner of the garden.

The brothers returned after a few days and were told of Chameli's death. They were shocked and saddened and they wept. But none of them suspected anything was wrong, for all the wives told them that Chameli could not bear the separation from her brothers and died from grief.

At the place where Chameli was buried grew a tall, elegant tree with beautiful silvery flowers that perfumed the air. The brothers loved the tree but their wives grew increasingly afraid of it. One day all six of them demanded that it be cut down.

They were so adamant about it that one of the brothers took an axe and was about to strike the tree when it said in a soft, gentle voice, "O brother, do not strike me. I am your Chameli."

The brothers turned to the frightened wives. The women then started accusing each other of ill-treating Chameli and the truth came out. The brothers embraced the tree and promised to care for it for the rest of their lives. And so the tree was named Neem Chameli.

It is an evergreen, straight, elegant tree with a narrow crown and drooping branchlets. Its yellowish grey bark is cracked and furrowed.

The leaves are divided into leaflets arranged in pairs along the main rib. These leaves are smooth and oval and each has a small leaflet at the end.

The flowers are beautiful, fragrant, snowy white masses at the ends of branchlets. Each flower is a slender tube sitting in a bell-shaped calyx. The petals are waxy white, sometimes flushed with a little pink. As they grow old they turn yellow.

The fruit is a long slender pod, pointed at both ends and containing flat seeds.

The wood is used for making small furniture.

20

SCREWPINE

Latin Names	*Pandanus tectorius,*
	Pandanus odoratissimus
English Name	*Screwpine*
Indian Names	*Bengali : Keya, Ketaki*
	Hindi : Kewra, Ketaki, Keora
	Kannada : Talemara
	Malayalam : Kaida
	Sanskrit : Ketaki
	Tamil : Thazhai
	Telugu : Mugali
Family	Pandanaceae

Pandanus is the Latinized form of the Malayan word
Pandan which means stickman and applies to all the
members of the screwpine family. *Tectorius* is the Latin
word for cover. *Odoratissimus* means full of fragrance.

The Keora is mentioned frequently in Tamil classics
as having flowers which neutralize with their strong
perfume the foul fish odour pervading the sea coast.
The flowers are swan-like in shape and are worn in the
hair. The plant is also used to fence in seaside villages.

Jehangir in his memoirs, *Tuzuk-i-Jahangiri*, describes the important flowers of India. About the Keora
flower he writes that its scent is so strong and penetrat-
ing that it even obscures that of musk.

One of the most beautiful Gujarat adivasi songs says:
Suraj ugyo re kevadiyani fanese
Chando surame re, Jhim jhagamaghe ho raat

The Sun rises behind the Kewra tree
The moon applies antimony to its eyes
The night is lit with soft moonlight.

Why the Ketaki is not worshipped

Millions of years ago, in Satyayuga, Vishnu performed a penance to attain eternal happiness. Brahma too performed a penance to annihilate all his desires.

One day, taking a break from their prayers, Vishnu and Brahma walked about in a forest where they met each other. A quarrel arose between them as to who was greater.

Suddenly Shiva came between them.

"I have a simple test", he said. "The first person to find either my head or my feet shall be greater than the other." He disappeared.

Vishnu and Brahma grew very agitated. Shiva had made his form so huge that they could not find his feet or his head.

Vishnu and Brahma decided to search in different directions. Vishnu became a boar and went to the lowest regions of Patalaloka. He dug up the earth furiously but he could not find Shiva's feet. Brahma got on to his swan and flew to the highest regions but he could not find Shiva's head.

Vishnu failed in his search and returned to the forest. As Brahma was coming back to the forest he saw a Ketaki flower falling from the sky. He decided to cheat in the contest.

Shiva wore a Ketaki flower on his forehead. Brahma caught the falling flower in his hand and took it to Vishnu.

"I have found Shiva's head", he claimed. "See, here is proof. I took the Ketaki flower from his forehead."

Vishnu did not believe him. He turned to the fragrant flower in Brahma's hand and asked, "Ketaki, is this true?"

The flower did not hesitate to brag. "Yes, my lord, I am indeed the flower on Shiva's forehead."

Immediately, even before Brahma had a chance to crow over his victory, Shiva appeared. He was angry, for he had heard the Ketaki lie. He stormed and cursed the flower. "O Ketaki, because you are a liar I do not want you to come near me. Even your flowers will not be allowed in my temples."

And so, even though the flowers of the Ketaki are wonderfully fragrant, no offering of them is ever made to Shiva.

A small gregarious tree. The stem is branched and rests on strong aerial roots. The leaves are sword-shaped, sharple-toothed and leathery, each one to two metres long and arranged spirally.

The male flowers grow in long white, very fragrant spathes. The female ones are short and yellow.

The fruit is a round mass of drupes, first yellow and then red when ripe.

The leaves of the Keora are woven into mats and are also used for making paper. The leaf fibre is used for fishing nets and lines and brush bristles. The aerial root fibre makes baskets, hats and brushes. Perfume from the male flowers is used in perfumes and in sweets. Keora is grown as a soil binder in the canals of Kerala.

21

POMEGRANATE

Latin Name	*Punica granatum*
English Name	Pomegranate
Indian Names	*Bengali : Dalim*
	Gujarati : Dadam
	Hindi : Anar
	Kannada : Dalimba
	Malayalam : Metalam
	Marathi : Dalimba
	Sanskrit : Dalima, Dadima
	Tamil : Madalai
	Telugu : Darimma
Family	Punicaceae

Pliny called it the Apple of Carthage, *Malum punicum*. The term means grain apple, a reference to the grain-like seeds within. Pomegranate comes from the French word *pome garnete* or seeded apple.

In Sanskrit there is an adage, 'dadima mani dansh', to bite the Pomegranate tree. This means a hard and unwelcome task.

The Pomegranate is a symbol of fertility and prosperity. The Pomegranate motif is found in temple carvings. Prophet Mohammad is said to have advised his followers to eat Pomegranates as a way to purge the spirit of envy.

The Parsis use its twigs to make their sacred broom. When a Parsi child is invested with the sacred thread, Pomegranate seeds are thrown over him to scare away evil spirits. Its juice is squeezed into the mouth of the dying.

The king and the gardener

Once on a hot summer day the king of the land, on a
visit to the distant parts of his realm, came to a garden.
The king was very thirsty. He got off his horse and
entered the garden gate. He saw a gardener tending
Pomegranate trees. Each tree was laden with fruit.

"May I have some Pomegranate juice?" asked the
king.

The gardener plucked a ripe Pomegranate fruit and
took it to his hut in the corner. In a few minutes a
beautiful maiden brought a cupful of fresh rich juice
for the king.

The king, his eyes dazzled by the girl's fair face,
drank the juice greedily. His thirst quenched, he looked
around the garden and saw fruit trees growing wild
everywhere.

"How much profit do you make from selling this
fruit?" he asked the gardener

"Three hundred dinars", replied the unsuspecting
gardener.

"And what do you pay the king's tax collector?"
asked the king.

"The king only takes one-tenth of the cultivated
grain. He does not take any money from the fruit",
answered the gardener.

The king saw the profusion of Pomegranate trees. "I
have so many trees all over my kingdom", he thought,
"I must start taxing orchards as well."

Pleased with his plan, the king decided to return
immediately to his capital. He swung onto his horse,
but before leaving, he asked for some more Pomegranate juice.

The old gardener had recognized his king but he pretended ignorance. He could almost see the thoughts passing through the king's mind as his eyes roved greedily over the Pomegranate trees. Both he and his daughter went back to the hut and came out with a cup. But this time the cup had only a few drops of juice in it. The king was puzzled.

"Where is the juice?" asked the king.

"My lord, when you asked for Pomegranate juice the first time, your heart was large and the Pomegranate gave of its juice freely. But now I have squeezed five Pomegranates and this is all I could get."

The king turned to the gardener.

"Can you explain this to me, gardener?" he asked.

"It is simple, my lord. Our king has a large heart. He lets the fruit grow wild and everyone partakes of it. The fruit knows it has his blessing, so it gives of its juice generously. Today, the fruit has felt that the king wishes to impose a tax on it. So it feels that the blessing has passed from it. And its juice has dried up."

The king felt ashamed of his greedy thoughts. He banished the idea of imposing a tax from his mind and his brow cleared. The gardener watched his mood change.

The king asked for more juice. This time his cup brimmed over with red juice. He thanked the gardener and his beautiful daughter and rode away.

It is a small, rounded, bushy tree. It has stiff, slender, spiny branches. The trunk is an erect red-brown which later turns grey. The tree has both evergreen and deciduous varieties.

The leaves are borne in clusters. They are small, narrow, lance-shaped, glossy and leathery. When young they are brownish green. This colour darkens as they age.

The vermilion-tinged orange flowers are broad. They have crumpled petals and a red, fleshy calyx which remains on the fruit. The flowers grow at the end of branches.

The fruit is a deep red berry. Its outer skin is hard and thick. Inside it has a great number of seeds, each in a small cell surrounded by carmine pink flesh. Once the fruit is ripe it splits open or laughs .

The fruit is eaten. Its seeds are dried and made into a condiment for curries. Every part of the tree has medicinal properties. The wood is used for agricultural implements.

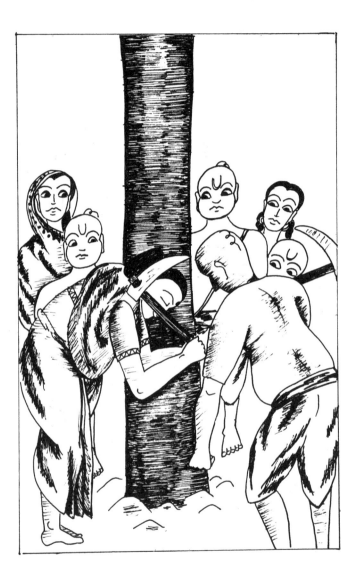

22

SESAME

Latin Name	*Sesamum indicum*
English Names	*Sesame, Benne Plant*
Indian Names	*Bengali : Til*
	Gujarati : Tal
	Hindi : Til
	Kannada : Ellu
	Malayalam : Karuthellu
	Marathi : Til
	Sanskrit : Tila
	Telugu : Nuvvulu
Family	Pedaliaceae

Sesamum comes from Sesamon, a name given by Hippocrates, after the Arabic word *Sesam* meaning herbs. Tila, in Sanskrit, means a small particle. The word Benne is from the Malayan word Bene.

It is supposed to have originated from Vishnu's sweat drops that fell on Earth. In the Vedas the nose is often called Tilapushpa or blossom of the Tila plant. The Atharva Veda mentions Sesame as a tree and field manure crop. It was also offered to the gods.

We hear of sesame seeds as far back as 3000 B. C. when the plant was a major source of food, wine and oil, and was guarded by royalty.

During the Vedic ages, it was the only oilseed used by the Aryans. The recovery of a lump of sesame at Harappa suggests that it was cultivated in the Indus Valley.

The farmer's house guest

One day Narayana (Vishnu) decided to visit the Earth to see how his people were doing. Lakshmi asked him if she could come along. Vishnu agreed on condition that while flying down to the Earth, she would not look northwards.

Of course, since he had forbidden her to look north, Lakshmi just had to look. She turned her head slightly and saw the Sesame flowers in the fields. Enchanted by the pretty white flowers she plucked them.

Narayana saw her hiding something. She showed them to him. Narayana said, "You do know, being a goddess, that it is a sin to take anything without the owner's permission. Now I shall have to punish you. You have caused the owner harm, so you will stay in his house for three years." And he carried on his tour.

Poor Lakshmi, confined to a mortal's body, went towards the owner's hut. The owner was a poor Brahmin with three sons and two daughters. He owned nothing save the small patch of land where he grew Sesame. The family earned just enough for one meal a day.

Lakshmi entered the house timidly. She was clad in rags. She told the Brahmin she had no place to stay. Could he give her shelter? Even though the Brahmin did not have enough for his own family, he agreed and Lakshmi took up abode there.

Luck came to the family, for Lakshmi is the goddess of luck. Their Sesame plants grew and they had twice the number of seeds. From that money they bought a cow and the cow gave enough milk to be sold. Slowly the family grew prosperous. The Brahmin shared his family's wealth with Lakshmi equally, as if she were a family member.

Two and a half years passed. The Brahmin built a new house, bought more land, bought more animals. He then said to his family, "All this has come to us from the gods. Let us go to the Ganges to thank them for our prosperity." The family decided to go on a pilgrimage.

Lakshmi refused to go. "I shall stay here and guard your house and fields", she said. The family embraced her and set off.

They came back months later. As their cart neared the house they saw a dazzling, resplendent woman get into a chariot studded with jewels. It was Lakshmi. Her three-year penance was over and Vishnu had come to fetch her.

The Brahmin realized it was her. He bowed his head in shame before her and apologized for not recognizing her and treating her the way a goddess should have been treated. But Lakshmi had been very happy these last three years. Blessing the Brahmin, she told him to look under the Bael tree as she had left a gift for him.

As soon as the goddess flew away, the family went to the Bael tree. A heap of gold and precious stones lay there, glittering. The Brahmin's family grew enormously rich and, because they never left their pious and generous ways, they lived happily ever after.

The Sesame plant is a tall, erect annual. The ovate leaves grow alternately up the stem and are deeply veined. The flowers are white and trumpet-shaped. Each grows singly in the axil of a leaf.

The fruit is a two celled pod with flattish pear-shaped seeds inside. When the seeds are ripe the pods burst open suddenly, like the Open Sesame of Ali Baba, and the seeds are scattered. The seeds vary in colour from yellowish white to black. Once they are peeled they are cream coloured.

Sesame seeds have a pleasant nutty flavour when roasted or fried and are used in bread, confectionery and Gajjak. Sesame oil is used as a cooking base.

23

PEEPAL

Latin Name	*Ficus religiosa*
English Names	*Bo Tree, Peepal Tree*
Indian Names	*Bengali : Asvattha*
	Gujarati : Jari
	Hindi : Pipal
	Malayalam : Avasai, Arasu
	Marathi : Ashwatha
	Sanskrit : Pippala, Ashvattha,
	Bodhadruma
	Telegu : Ashvatthame
Family	Moraceae

Ficus means fig and *religiosa* shows that it is venerated. The Sanskrit word Ashvattha means under which horses stand. Bodhadruma means the tree of perfect wisdom. The name Pipal has an interesting origin. The Pipal tree has a resemblance to the Poplar tree in that its leaves also shake. Aryan immigrants, seeing the tree for the first time, gave it the name of the Poplar or Pappel, a tree they were familiar with in the northern latitudes. Even now in Italy the transplanted Pipal is called Populo delle Indie or the Indian Poplar. In the earlier discriptions of Indian flora it was called the Poplar-leaved fig tree.

The Pipal is the oldest depicted tree in India. In Vedic times it was used to make fire by friction.

Considered a sacred tree, the Pipal is seldom cut. It is associated with the Triad, the roots being Brahma, the stem Vishnu and each leaf being the seat of a minor

god. The Ashvattha Stotra says: "I bow to the sacred Fig Tree, to Brahma in the root, to Vishnu in the trunk and to Shiva in the foliage". In another myth Vishnu was born under a Pipal and is therefore considered the tree itself. Yet another legend has Shiva and Parvati talking and playing together when the other gods eavesdrop. An enraged Parvati curses all of them to be reborn as trees. Brahma becomes the Palasa, Rudra the Ficus indica and Vishnu the Pipal.

The Pipal is considered a Brahmin tree and Brahmins offer prayers under it. In Gujarat it is considered a Brahmin itself and invested with the sacred triple cord. It is considered that one who cuts it has murdered a Brahmin and his family will soon become extinct. It is served with food offerings when a male member of the family dies.

Some communities believe that the spirits of the dead do not get water in the next world. The Pipal is considered a pathway. So water is poured on its roots on three days of the dark half of Kartik (mid-October to mid-November) and Shravana (mid-July to mid-August) and on the 14th day of the bright half of Chaitra (March-end).

The Pipal is often married to the Nim or the Banana. If the trees grow togther they are considered husband and wife. On Amavasya, the last day of the dark half of the month, particularly if it is a Monday, villagers worship these trees and perform a symbolic marriage between them. After the threads are tied, they circle the trees 108 times to remove all their sins.

Manasa, the goddess of serpents, worshipped in Bengal, is said to live in this tree.

Krishna was shot by a hunter's arrow while he sat under the Pipal tree.

The Pipal is sacred to the Buddhists as Prince Siddhartha received enlightenment under it in Bodh Gaya and became the Buddha. Hence it is also called the Bodhi tree or Tree of Enlightenment. The Chinese traveller Hiuen Tsang gives an account of this tree. In the olden days, he says, when Buddha was alive, this tree was several hundred feet high. Often injured by cutting or breaking for relics, it is now only 50 feet high. Buddha reached perfect wisdom under it, so it is called the Samyak Sambodhi or Tree of Knowledge. The bark is yellowish white, the leaves dark green. The leaves remain shining and glossy the whole year. But on Nirvana Day they wither and hang their heads, then in a little while revive as before. On this day of Nirvana many princes assemble and bathe the roots of the tree with scented perfume and milk and offer it gifts.

The Pipal tree in Sri Lanka is believed to be 2147 years old. It was believed that the ruling dynasty of Buddhists would last as long as the tree survived and for this reason it was well looked after.

In Purabi, the dialect of eastern Uttar Pradesh, there is a saying used when expelling evil spirits or when talking of someone's evil temper. It goes :

Je Jagdipen nagar ujaaral, raakas chhoral pipar
Se Jagdipa aawat baru, haathe le le musar.

Jagdipa, who made the town desolate and from whom even the demon fled the Pipal, is now coming with a pestle in her hand.

Jagdipa was, in folklore, an exceedingly quarrelsome woman. She fought with everyone in the village, all the time. She abused and hit them and made life so unpleasant that the villagers started leaving the village and settling down elsewhere.

138

One day there was no one left to quarrel with. Jagdipa was undaunted. She picked up her broom and attacked the Pipal tree, shouting abuse at it all the while. The demon in the tree, no faintheart himself, stood it for a few days. But finally even his nerve gave way and he rushed away from the tree and sought refuge elsewhere.

How the Pipal saved King Jarasandha's kingdom
(Folk tale from the Kahars of Bihar)

King Jarasandha built a garden and tower at Giriak on the northern border of the Ganga district. The area was affected by drought and the garden withered. In desperation King Jarasandha offered his daughter and half his kingdom to anyone who could bring water straight from the Ganga and water his garden in one night.

The Chief of the Kahars built a great embankment and made a long rope from the Bawan Ganga, a rivulet of the main river, to the garden. He dipped swing baskets into the water and sent them down the rope to the garden where his tribesmen emptied the baskets throughout the garden.

Jarasandha then changed his mind. He did not want to marry his royal daughter to a Kahar, a labourer in the fields. Even more, he did not want to part with his kingdom. He sat under his Pipal tree and despaired.

Suddenly the Pipal tree turned into a cock and crowed loudly. The Kahars thought it was morning and stopped work. They thought the king would take vengeance on them for presuming to take his daughter and half his kingdom. So they fled, leaving a small portion of the garden unwatered.

King Jarasandha could afford to be magnanimous now that his garden, daughter and kingdom had been saved by the Pipal tree. He called the Kahars back and assured them that, while they had lost the wager, he would pay them for their night's work. He paid them three and a half seers of grain and this has been their daily wages since then.

Bhima's trial of strength

(A Muria tribal legend)

Mahaprabhu made men, animals and trees. Men increased in number and strength and started making villages. To maintain order, Mahaprabhu made Chalika the king of men and Chalika made a government to help him rule. Mahaprabhu made a chief and watchman for every village.

Then the animals increased. Mahaprabhu made a king and watchmen for them too.

One day the trees assembled on Hemagiri mountain and complained, "You have made a government for all but us. We have no one to defend us, no one to protect us."

Bhima was passing by. "Why are all the trees together?" he asked himself. He hurried to the top of Hemagiri mountain and asked the trees why they had assembled. They told him their problem.

"I will see who the strongest is", decided Bhima. He pushed each tree and each tree fell over except the Tamarind, the Pipal and the Banyan. Bhima told Mahaprabhu about the test he had taken.

Mahaprabhu came down to Hemagiri mountain. He made the Tamarind the King, the Banyan which spread its branches everywhere and so could get more information from around the Earth, he made the Minister. And he made the Pipal the watchman. "Whenever the wind blows or a storm approaches, you will warn the other trees."

And that is why the leaves of the Pipal rustle in the wind.

It is a very large tree. The bark is light grey and smooth and peels in patches.

The young branches are smooth and shiny. The long leaves grow on long stalks and are a shiny dark red when young. They are smooth, leathery, heart-shaped tapering at the apex into a long tail. The leaves hang down and the slightest breeze makes them tremble and rustle.

The flowers are inconspicuous and colourless and are hidden by the figs when they emerge in pairs between the leaf-stalk and the branch. At first the fruit is green and smooth and then turns purple when ripe. The figs are eaten by birds and bats. Each part of the tree is used in ayurvedic medicine. The leaves are fed to camels and elephants. The bark contains tannin and is sometimes used for tanning leather and to make a red dye.

24

SACRED BASIL

Latin Name	*Ocimum sanctum*
English Name	*Sacred Basil*
Indian Names	*Bengali : Tulasi*
	Hindi : Tulasi, Vrinda
	Kannada : Vishnu tulsi
	Malayalam : Trittairu
	Marathi : Tulasa
	Sanskrit : Manjari
	Tamil : Thulasi
	Telugu : Brinda, Gaggera
Family	Labiatae

Ocimum comes from the Greek word Ocymum, meaning sweet herbs. *Sanctum* is Holy. Tulasi means matchless. Vrinda means a cluster or multitude of flowers.

In the olden days temples served as rest houses for travellers. The Tulasi plant was grown outside the temples because it has the unique property of curbing thirst. A couple of leaves under the tongue and the weary traveller, looking for water, would feel less thirsty. In time it was forgotten that the Tulasi was planted near temples for this reason, and the plant acquired a religious significance.

It became essential in the worship of Hindu gods and goddesses, especially Vishnu. According to the Padma Purana even the soil around the Tulasi plant is holy. The soul of a dead person whose body had been cremated with Tulasi sticks attains a permanent place in Vishnu's heaven and is not reborn. If a lamp is built for

Vishnu's worship with a single Tulasi twig it is equivalent to several million lamps.

Tulasi is Lakshmi, Vishnu's consort, in many incarnations on the Earth. Tulasi is considered an incarnation of Radha, Krishna's beloved. Radha's name is also Vrinda and the Mathura forest where Krishna played in his childhood with her is Vrindavana or the Garden of Radha or Tulasi, hence the name of Tulasi as Vrinda. Every November, the 12th day of the first half of the month Kartika, is Tulasi Divas when the plant is ceremonially married to Krishna.

The plant is also called the Little Shrub Goddess and is a symbol of devotion and surrender. The belief still exists today that a Tulasi plant is essential to a home to ensure happiness. Tulasivrindavana is the name of the square pedestal planted with Tulasi before the doors of a Hindu house.

The Aryan myth is one of a woman devotee of Vishnu called Tulasi who desired the god as her husband. She prayed for centuries. Lakshmi, the consort of Vishnu, unable to bear the idea of a rival, changed Tulasi into a plant. But Vishnu, impressed by the woman's devotion and angry with Lakshmi, assumed the form of the Shaligrama or Ammonite stone and said that he would be Tulasi's consort eternally. The two, the plant and the stone, are married annually. From this legend grew the later legend of Tulasi.

How Lakshmi became Tulasi

(Devi Bhagavata)

Sarasvati, Ganga and Lakshmi were, in the beginning, all wives of Vishnu and he loved them equally. One day the three quarrelled and Sarasvati cursed Lakshmi to be reborn as a plant on Earth. Then both Ganga and Sarasvati cursed each other into becoming rivers on Earth.

When the whole tumult was over, seeing that Lakshmi had got the worst of it, Vishnu took her aside and told her, "Don't worry, Devi. Things have happened as predestined. You will be born as the daughter of Dharmadhvaja and then you will be transformed into a plant sacred enough to make all three worlds pure. When you are Tulasi, a demon named Shankhachuda, who is a part of me, will marry you and you will come back to me."

King Dharmadhvaja was a devotee of Lakshmi. Lakshmi entered his wife Madhavi's womb and after a hundred years she was born. She was fully grown at the time of birth, and being extremely beautiful was called Tulasi or the Matchless. She had no memory of being Lakshmi, all she knew was that she felt a fierce love for Vishnu.

Tulasi did not stay in the palace of her parents. She went to Badrikashrama and prayed for twenty-four thousand years for Vishnu to become her husband. She sat on hot coals in summer and in icy water in winter and she ate only fruit. Then she prayed for another thirty thousand years, eating only leaves, another forty thousand on air alone and another ten thousand, holding her breath.

The gods were taken aback by her austerity. Brahma appeared before her and said, "Devi, you know that the cowherd Sudama, born as a friend of Krishna, was actually a part of Vishnu himself. He was cursed by Radha and has now been reborn as the demon Shankhachuda. He has fallen in love with you. Marry him now and later you can become the wife of Vishnu."

Tulasi agreed.

Shankhachuda had obtained a boon from the gods that Tulasi would marry him, and that he would be immortal as long as his wife remained faithful and chaste. The demon, knowing of Tulasi's austerity, was certain that he would live forever. He married her and, as the years went by, he became increasingly arrogant. He started annoying the lesser gods and they went to Vishnu to complain.

Vishnu sent Shiva to kill Shankhachuda. Shiva entered the forest and challenged the demon to a battle. He lured Shankhachuda away.

In the meantime, Vishnu disguised himself as Shankhachuda and entered Tulasi's house. Tulasi received him with great love and the two lay down together. But Tulasi grew suspicious of the impostor and she sprang up to curse him when Vishnu revealed himself in his true form. "You have been praying for thousands of years to get me as your husband", he said. "Now Shankhachuda will have been killed, for you have been unfaithful to him. It is time for him to regain his form as Sudama and come back to me. For you too, the time has come to be Lakshmi again."

Vishnu continued,"Your body will turn into the river Gandaki. Your hair will become the Tulasi plant which will be held sacred in all three worlds."

Tulasi resumed her form as Lakshmi and went back to Vishnu's world Vaikuntha with her husband.

How Krishna was saved from slavery

Narada, the mischievous sage, was on another visit to Satyabhama, the wife of Krishna. He found her in a pensive mood.

"What is the matter, daughter?" asked Narada. "What in the world troubles that pretty head of yours?"

"Muni", started Satyabhama, "Krishna is my husband in this life. But when I die and am reborn, I could be someone else's wife, couldn't I?"

"That is so, Satyabhama", answered the sage gravely, but a twinkle came into his eye, for he could see where the conversation was leading.

But Satyabhama's eyes had filled with tears. "But I don't want anyone but Krishna", she exclaimed. "Is there no way that I can make sure I will be Krishna's wife in every birth?"

Narada pretended to think. Then he sat up and looked as if he had hit upon a solution. "There is one sure way, daughter", he said. "The laws of time and rebirth say that anything given to a Brahmin in charity will be returned to the giver in all future births. Now if you give me Krishna you are sure to get him back each time and without all his other wives!"

Satyabhama was both innocent and impulsive. She saw this as the ideal solution. She sent her maid to call Krishna and when her husband appeared, she said to Narada grandly, "Muni, I donate my husband Krishna to you in charity."

Krishna was taken by surprise. But before he could say anything Narada said, "Now Krishna, you have been donated to me by your wife. From today you will be my servant. You will cook and clean and gather firewood and accompany me on my travels. Come, let us depart. I have much ground to cover." He picked up his staff and made as if to go out of the palace door.

Krishna knew he could not refuse. The rules of charity were inflexible. He cast a hunted look around him. "May I say goodbye to the rest of the household, O Master?" he asked Narada.

"All right", agreed the sage. "And change your clothes too. Wear something more suitable for a servant."

Krishna went into the hallway. But Satyabhama's maids had already informed all his wives of Krishna's predicament. They crowded round him wailing. "I cannot do anything", Krishna said. "You will have to ask Narada Muni."

The wives rushed to Narada and begged him to release their husband from bondage. Even Satyabhama had realized what she had done and she joined the others in their pleas.

Narada enjoyed the household's predicament. Krishna stood by quietly, a strange smile on his face. "You know, ladies, that it is a sin to receive anything in charity from a Brahmin. So I cannot condemn your souls to eternal damnation by gifting Krishna back to you. However . . ." and Narada scratched his head and appeared lost in thought, "you may buy him back from me if you give me his weight in gold."

The wives shouted in glee and each rushed off to her chamber to fetch her ornaments. A large scale was called for and Krishna sat on one side of the scale. On the other lay a growing pile of gold jewellery.

The heap grew and grew but the scale did not tilt even slightly. The wives tore off the jewellery they were wearing and stood with bare necks and arms, but the scale remained weighted down on Krishna's side. Soon there was no more gold in the palace. The wives went to the goldsmith and traded their possessions for gold but even that amount did not help. They grew frantic with worry.

Then Rukmini, who was the calmest of the wives, went inside her room. She went to her garden. In the centre of the garden grew a Tulasi plant which both Krishna and Rukmini watered every day. She plucked a leaf of the Tulasi plant and brought it to the huge heap of ornaments on the scale.

Rukmini placed the tiny Tulasi leaf on top. Immediately the scale shifted and Krishna's side went up. The wives stood still in wonder. "Why?" they asked in unison. "When our ornaments did not make any difference, being so heavy, how did a small Tulasi leaf tilt the balance?"

Rukmini looked at Krishna and all her knowledge of his past lives as Vishnu was in her eyes. She knew that Radha, his beloved, was the Tulasi plant. "But Tulasi has always been his most beloved wife", she said gently. "A leaf offered by her is more than any gold that we can put. Is that not so, my lord?" And Krishna smiled at Rukmini's wisdom.

And so Krishna was saved from servitude and Narada went off to create trouble elsewhere.

It is a small, many branched, erect and hairy plant. The leaves have toothed margins and are hairy on both surfaces. They are dotted with minute oil glands and when crushed give a strong fragrant scent.

The flowers are small, purplish and grow in slender spiked clusters.

The fruit is small and the seeds are yellow-red.

The Tulasi plant has medicinal leaves and seeds, the juice of both being a remedy for coughs and colds and digestive problems. The oil of the leaves destroys bacteria and keeps away insects. The plant is an effective fly and mosquito repellent.

25

INDIAN LOTUS

Latin Names	*Nelumbo nucifera*
	Nelumbium speciosum
English Names	*Indian Lotus, Egyptian Bean*
Indian Names	*Gujarati : Suryakamala*
	Hindi : Kamala, Padma, Saroja
	Malayalam : Thamara
	Marathi : Kamal
	Punjabi : Kanwal, Pamposh
	Sanskrit : Padma, Kamala,
	Abja, Saroja
	Tamil : Tamarai
	Telugu : Kalung
Family	Nymphaeaceae

Nelumbum means water bean, lotus. It is neo-Latin, coming from the Singhalese Nelumbu. The word Lotus is from the Greek Lotos. The Sanskrit words Abja and Saroja mean waterborne. Kamala means rosy and desirous. It also means excellence.

In Hindu mythology the lotus is the cradle of the universe. When the deluge swept away all matter, Vishnu lay upon the waters and a lotus flowered from his navel. Brahma, the Creator, emerged from it and created the world. One of Brahma's names is Sarojin or of the lotus. Another is Kanja, the lotus. The pre-Aryan cult of the Mother Goddess was adopted by the Aryan Hindus and the goddess Shree or Lakshmi, the consort of Vishnu, is associated with the lotus. Lotus-born, standing on a lotus, lotus-coloured, lotus-eyed, decked with lotus garlands are some of her descriptions. In a medallion in Stupa II at Sanchi, Shree is shown standing on a lotus in the middle of a lotus lake. Lakshmi, enthroned on the Lotus of knowledge, is Kamala and Padma. In Vedic mythology when the Ocean of Milk was churned by the gods and asuras, she sprang from the waves, a lotus in her hand.

Vishnu holds a lotus in one hand. This lotus represents the universe, the flower that unfolds in all its glory from the formless endlessness of the causal waters.

The Vedas speak of the inner core of man's being where the spirit dwells as being lotus-shaped. The heart, the abode of god, is referred to as Hridayakamalam, the lotus of the heart.

The lotus grows out of mud but its beauty is undefiled. It is compared by Hindus and Buddhists to a good man who remains unaffected by the wickedness of the world. One of the Puranas is the Padmapurana.

Few flowers have an older symbolism. The rose-coloured lotus of the Dal Lake in Srinagar is the symbol of sunrise. The Mughals based the designs of their fountains on the lotus bud.

The sun and lotus interdependence is a symbol of eternal love. In early mythology the sun was Vishnu and the lotus Lakshmi, his consort. The lotus awakening and blooming at the first rays of the morning sun is a recurrent theme in Indian literature. One of the names of the sun is the Friend of the Lotus. Even today the lotus is the main offering to Surya, the Sun god. From the *Hitopadesha*, the Book of Good Counsels, comes this verse:

The people are the lotus leaves, their monarch is the Sun.

When he doth sink beneath the waves, they vanish
every one.
When he doth rise they rise again, with bud and
blossom rife
To bask awhile in his warm smile, who is their lord
and life.

Beautiful women are likened in literature to every
part of the lotus. Treatises classify women into four
types of beauty of which the highest is Padmini, the
Lotus Lady whose very breath contains the fragrance
of the lotus.

How Lakshmi saved the devas
(Devi Bhagavata)

Once the Devas or lesser gods were cursed by the Sage
Durvasa to become old and poor. Indra lost his majesty
and was ousted from Svargaloka. The guardian goddess
of his kingdom Svargalakshmi deserted it and went to
Vaikuntha where she merged with Vishnu's consort
Mahalakshmi.

The Devas were extremely unhappy with their condition. They went to Satyaloka, the kingdom of
Brahma, and appealed to Brahma to restore their
youth, looks and wealth. But Brahma said he was
helpless in the face of such a strong curse.

So the Devas went to Vaikuntha. Mahavishnu
smiled when he heard their grievances. He turned to
Mahalakshmi and said, "You are the only one who can
help the Devas with your powers. Go and take birth as
Kshirasagarakanyaka (Daughter of the Ocean of
Milk)."

Accordingly, the Devas started churning the Ocean
of Milk. Soon Mahalakshmi, seated on a lotus and

holding one in her hand, emerged from the churning waters and blessed the Devas. Kamala, for that means from the lotus, put a garland of lotus flowers round Mahavishnu's neck and was reunited with him in Vaikuntha.

The Devas got back their wealth and youth and they worshipped Lakshmi from then on as their Goddess of Fortune.

How Bhima found Hanuman
(Mahabharata)

Draupadi once asked her husband Bhima to get for her the celestial lotus of a thousand petals. The lotus, with its sunlike splendour and heavenly fragrance, was supposed to prolong life and renew one's beauty.

Bhima set out to find the flower. On the way he saw a monkey lying in his path. Bhima said, "Monkey, remove yourself from my way."

The monkey replied indolently, "I will only get up if you pick up my tail."

Thinking the monkey to be just another irritant which could be easily removed, Bhima strode forward and grasped his tail. He gave it a mighty tug, intending to throw the monkey far into the forest.

But the tail did not even move. Bhima tugged and pulled and pushed but the tail lay supine on the ground and the monkey yawned with boredom.

Finally the sweat-stained Bhima gave up. "Who are you, monkey?" he asked tiredly. "this is no ordinary body."

Then Hanuman drew himself up to his proper height. "I am Hanuman, the son of the Wind god Pavana", he announced mightily.

"But so am I!" exclaimed Bhima. "We must be brothers."

They hugged each other. "Why are you in this forest?" asked Hanuman. "Where are you going?"

Bhima explained that he was searching for the celestial lotus for Draupadi.

"Leave it to me", said Hanuman. He flew away and after a while, returned with the lotus and gave it to Draupadi.

Indra's hiding place

Once in mythological times, the demons or Asuras declared war on Indra, the chief of the gods. They attacked in strength and Indra was defeated and dethroned. In shame he fled to the nether regions of Patalalok and hid himself in the stem of a lotus flower.

Indra's wife Sachi hunted for her husband everywhere. But he was nowhere to be found. Worried, she prayed to Vishnu.

Vishnu mustered the gods together, fought the demons and defeated them. He then went to Patalaloka and brought Indra back and seated him on his throne.

Gajendra and the crocodile
(Bhagavata Purana)

On the Trikuta mountain lived Gajendra, the Lord of the Elephants. Like all elephants, he liked bathing in the water. One day, roaming around the mountain, he found a new pool and heaved himself into the water.

Suddenly a giant crocodile emerged from the muddy bottom and seized Gajendra's leg. The elephant thrashed and fought but he sank slowly into the water.

"Vishnu, save me", he called out despairingly.

Vishnu heard his cry and appeared. But the elephant felt that his last hour had come. Before he sank into the water, he pulled a lotus flower and offered it to Vishnu with his trunk as his last act in life.

Vishnu, touched at the devotion of Gajendra, seized the crocodile's huge jaws and unclamped them from the leg. Gajendra climbed out of the pool and was saved.

Indra the thief
(Mahabharata)

The Sage Agastya was renowned for his discourses but he very rarely gave them, and certainly not when he was asked. One day the god Indra led a group of hermits on a pilgrimage. On their way, the pilgrims passed by Brahmasaras where Agastya lived and Indra was seized by a sudden desire to listen to a discouse from the reticent sage.

Agastya had planted lotus flowers round his hermitage. Indra and the other sages plucked all the flowers that Agastya had tended so carefully and ate them.

The sage came to know of the theft when he returned from the forest to his hermitage. He pursued the pilgrims and when he caught up with them, he identified Indra as the thief. Agastya launched into a long diatribe about duty and morals. Indra listened in satisfaction. When Agastya had finished Indra said, "O Sage, had it not been for my eagerness to hear a discourse on duty from you I would not have stolen your lotus flowers." So saying, he made the flowers appear again in the hermitage. Agastya was pleased and let Indra and the hermits depart in peace.

The lotus is a water plant. The bluish-green, waxy leaf is large and round with a stout cylindrical stalk arising from the centre. The plant exudes a milky sap.

The flowers, ranging from white to deep pink and red grow well above water level and are large with each petal being concave and veined. The seed heads of the lotus are like the nose of a watering can, embedded in a swollen receptacle.

The roots and seeds are eaten, the latter being used as a heart stimulant. The lotus went from India to Egypt in about 50 B.C.

26

POPPY

Latin Name	*Papaver somniferum*
English Name	*Poppy*
Indian Names	*Bengali : Posto*
	Hindi : Post, Aphim
	Kannada : Biligasgase, Afin
	Malayalam : Kashakhasa
	Marathi : Aphu
	Sanskrit : Aphenam
	Tamil : Kasa-kasa
Family	Papaveraceae

Papaver is Latin for Poppy. *Somniferum* means bringing sleep. Aphena in Sanskrit means frothless or without scum.

How Postomoni became the opium plant

On the banks of the river Ganga lived a Rishi. He shared his small palm-leaved hut with a small mouse. The two became companions.

One day the mouse, sitting in the Rishi's lap, said, "Holy sage, may I ask you for a boon?"

"Of course", answered the Rishi, puzzled as to what a mouse could want. "Do you want more food?"

"Oh no", assured the mouse. "You see, I am always being chased by cats. I have no defence against them. Please make me a cat so that I am their equal."

The Rishi sprinkled some water on the mouse and it turned into a cat which bounded off happily.

A few days later, the cat came into the hut, its fur all torn. "Rishi", it mewed. "I have a new enemy. The dog. Please make me a dog so that I can combat him."

The Rishi again sprinkled some water over the cat and it turned into a dog, which ran away barking ferociously.

A few days passed. The Rishi was at his meditation when a thin, woe-begone dog came and lay at his feet. "Sage, I have not eaten for many days. As a dog, I do not know where to get my food. I envy the monkeys who live off the fruit from the trees."

The Rishi was amused. With some more water he turned the dog into a monkey.

The monkey leapt from tree to tree. Joyfully it ate the fruit off the branches.

Summer came by and it became very hot. The monkey, sitting on its tree, found it difficult to find water and it was thirsty and hot all the time. "How I envy the wild boar, splashing about in the lake", it thought.

The Rishi, sitting under the tree, understood the thoughts of the monkey. He turned it into a wild boar. The boar went straight into the water and rolled happily in the mud.

Two days later the king was out hunting wild boar. The king rode on his elephant and he and his men threw spears at the boar. Our boar just escaped being killed. It limped back to the Rishi.

"This is a very dangerous life", it complained. "How I wish I was as big and strong as an elephant." The Rishi made the boar an elephant.

The wild elephant was caught in time by the king's men. It was kept in the royal stables and it hated losing its freedom. One day, the king and queen mounted it and went to bathe in the Ganga. The elephant was eager to see the Rishi and as it neared the banks of the river, it leapt about so violently that the queen fell off. The king caught her in his arms and kissed her.

The elephant ran to the Rishi and slumped to its knees. "O Rishi", it said, tears falling from its eyes. "Of all the creatures in the world a Queen must be the happiest. Please grant me this last boon and make me a Queen."

"How can I make you a Queen?" asked the Rishi. "A Queen needs a King and a kingdom. All I can do is to change you to a beautiful girl and you can capture the heart of a prince yourself."

The elephant became the beautiful maiden Postomoni. She lived with the Rishi and took care of him. One day a richly clad stranger came to the hut. "I have been hunting", he said. "And I am thirsty. Please, may I have some water and fruit."

Postomoni gave him both. He was the king of a nearby kingdom and he fell in love with the pretty girl. He took her away to his kingdom and married her. Postomoni forgot the sage. She did not thank him, she did not even call him for her wedding.

The sage was very hurt. In irritation, he cast a spell on her. A few days after her wedding Postomoni, standing near a well, felt giddy, fell into the well and died.

The king went broken-hearted to the sage who by now was sorry for what he had done.

"Do not grieve, king", he said. "The Queen was born a mouse who became a cat, a dog, a monkey, a boar, an elephant and finally your wife. Now I will make her immortal. Let her body remain in the well. Fill up the well with mud. A plant will grow from her flesh and bones and it will be called Posto or Poppy."

"This flower will produce opium", continued the sage. "Men will take it greedily. Whosoever partakes of it will have one quality of each of these animals into which Postomoni was transformed. He will be as mischievous as a mouse, as fond of milk as a cat, as quarrelsome as a dog, as unclean as a monkey, as savage as a boar, as strong as an elephant and as spirited as a Queen."

The king went back and did as the sage had said. In time a tall plant with delicate white leaves grew. The king looked after Postomoni. Every year he planted her seeds in the fields around as his children, so that by the time he died, there were hundreds of poppy flowers all over the kingdom.

The poppy plant grows annually. It has stout stalks and large grey-green irregularly-toothed smooth leaves which are clasped at the base.

The nodding flowers are large and showy, varying in colour from white, pink, red, violet, red, to purple. The flowers stay only a short while.

The fruit is a large, globe-shaped capsule which contains lots of very small kidney-shaped seeds. Like the flower the colour of the seeds varies. The Somniferum poppy or white poppy has white seeds.

Poppy seeds have a pleasing nut-like taste and are used on confectionery and bread. The seeds have a very high protein content. Poppy seed oil is used in cooking. From the half-ripened poppy seed capsules comes opium used in medicine and as a narcotic.

SAL TREE

Latin Name	*Shorea robusta*
English Name	*Sal Tree*
Indian Names	*Bengali : Sal*
	Hindi : Sal, Sekuva
	Malayalam : Maramaram
	Marathi : Rala
	Oriya : Sagua
	Punjabi : Sal, Seral
	Sanskrit : Shala, Deerghaphala
	Tamil : Kungiliyam
	Telugu : Gugul

Family	Dipterocarpaceae

Shorea is named after Dr Charles W. Shore, a Kentucky botanist. *Robusta* means stout. Gugal in Telegu means resin as does Rala in Marathi. The Sanskrit word Shala means rampart.

The Sal is considered a sacred tree by the tribals who consider it the home of spirits and build their shrines under its shade. The Bagdis and Bauris of Bengal are married under an arbour made of its branches. In the villages,the Sal tree, when it is in full bloom, is worshipped by childless couples for offspring.

The Sal is one of the trees revered by Buddhists, for it is associated with the birth and death of Gautama Buddha. It is said that, at the time of his birth in 563 BC, his mother Queen Mahamaya seized the branch of a great Sal tree. Buddha died in a Sal grove. In the

Jatakas or legends of the previous lives of the Buddha, tree spirits play a great part and are worshipped with perfume, flowers and food. They are depicted as dwelling in many trees but their particular favourites are the Sal, the Semul and the Banyan.

The devotee's dream
(Folk tale from Gujarat)

In Baravala, Gujarat, there is a small shrine of Bhimnatha Mahadeva. It nestles in the shade of a huge Sal tree. A devotee worshipped there every day and prayed to become rich. His wish was granted and, through a series of miraculous happenings, he became extremely wealthy.

The devotee was joyous. He wanted to show his gratitude to Bhimanatha Mahadeva. "What a small, ugly shrine such a powerful god has", he thought. "The least I can do is to make a grand temple of brick and stone and paint it so that everyone can see his glory." He called the temple builders and they told him that they would have to cut down the Sal tree to build the temple in its full glory. "Yes, yes, cut it down", said the rich man impatiently. "We must have the temple soon."

So the masons and the labourers and the artisans got ready and a woodsman was called the next day to chop down the tree. But the rich man tossed restlessly on his bed that night. Bhimnatha Mahadeva appeared to him in a dream and his face was stern. "What need have I", he thundered, "to sit in your closed airless temples? I am the spirit of this tree. It is my home and the home of many gods who live here with me. Will you cut it down to honour me foolishly? Is that how you repay me for making you rich?" "No, my Lord", cringed the rich man, "I am sorry. I did not know."

The temple building was called off. The small shrine stands under the Sal till today and after the devotees worship Bhimnatha Mahadeva they offer flowers to the Sal tree too.

It is a large tree with a thick rough dark grey bark. The young branches are covered with a greyish velvet.

The leaves are large, smooth, broadly ovate and shiny.

The flowers are yellowish with orange hearts with the outside of their petals covered in greyish velvet.

The fruit is ovoid and each has one seed.

The wood is hard and durable and used for bridge construction, railway coaches, boats, furniture and cart wheels. The bark is used for tanning and the gum makes soft wax harder in shoe polish.

The seed oil is valuable because, after processing, it substitutes for cocoa butter in the manufacture of chocolate.

28

MARIGOLD

Latin Name	*Tagetes erecta*
English Name	*Marigold*
Indian Names	*Bengali : Gaenda*
	Gujarati : Guljharu, Makhanala
	Hindi : Gaenda
	Kannada : Seemeshamantige
	Marathi : Zendu, Rajia-cha-plul
	Sanskrit : Sthulapushpa
	Tamil : Tulukkasamandi
	Telugu : Bantichettu
Family	Compositae

Tagetes is the Latin from Tages, an Etruscan god who is supposed to have emerged from a furrow, thereby becoming a child of Earth. He represents a youth who has the wisdom of age. *Erecta* means straight.

Hairpin flower
(Tribal tale from the Konds of Koraput)

Kondmuli Deota was the god of the Konds. He lived on Borandi Hill. One day he fell in love with a woman already married to another god.

Kondmuli stole her away from her home and brought her to his hill. The husband searched frantically for his wife and finally he spotted her on Borandi Hill.

The husband led an army of gods to attack Kondmuli Deota. In the battle that followed, Kondmuli's head was

cut off. The husband tied up his wife and dragged her away. As she left weeping, she took a hairpin from her hair and threw it on the hill in memory of Kondmuli. The pin took root in the ground and turned into the Marigold flower.

It is a robust, stiff annual. The leaves are deeply cut with each pinnae dissected. The leaves have a strong scent. The flowers are large and foamy. It grows to about two feet high.

An infusion of the plant is used to relieve rheumatism and bronchitis. The flowers are used for eye diseases. The flowers are offered as garlands and used in religious ceremonies.

29

HIBISCUS

Latin Name	*Hibiscus (the second name is on the variety of which there are hundreds)*
English Names	*Hibiscus, China Rose*
Indian Names	*Bengali : Jaba* *Gujarati : Jasuva* *Hindi : Javakusum, Jasud, Juva, Gudhal* *Marathi : Jasavanda* *Sanskrit : Japa, Javakusum* *Tamil : Semparuthi* *Telugu : Javapushpamu*
Family	Malvaceae

The word *Hibiscus* comes from the Greek word *Ebiskos* used by Dioscorides to name the Mallow. The name Java or Jaba is Japa in Sanskrit and means prayer.

The petals were used to blacken shoes, so the English name Shoeflower was given.

The Charak festival is celebrated in Bengal in April. Devotees do penance for their sins and have their skin pierced by thin short arrows that have the Jaba flower stuck at the ends.

The goddess' flower
(Devi Bhagavata)

The Hibiscus is dedicated to the goddess Durga. How did this happen?

According to a legend in the Devi Bhagavata, Jasun was an ardent devotee of the Devi. When the gods asked the Devi to assume the form of Kali to destroy evil, Jasun donated the red colour of her flowers to the goddess Kali's eyes so that she could show her anger.

Kali was pleased with her devotee's sacrifice. She told Jasun to ask her for any favour and it would be granted. "I wish to serve you forever", asked Jasun humbly.

"You shall be my flower", granted the Devi. "From today you will be known by many names: Jathon, Deviphool, Jabakusum. Whoever gives me an offering of your flowers shall be blessed by me." Since then the Hibiscus flower is offered by devotees to Kali.

There are over 200 varieties of the plant in India. The most common one is *Hibiscus rosa chinensis* or China Rose. It is a shrub, which sometimes grows as high as a small tree. The branches are woody and rather coarse. The bright green leaves grow alternately. They are broadly ovate in shape and sharply toothed along their margins. Both leaf and stem are covered with fine hair.

The flowers are of all colours, from white to purple, and every year new combinations are grown, yellow with pink hearts, peach with orange hearts. Some of them are single and other double varieties. The flowers are bell-shaped, short-stalked and solitary. They have a long stamen. Each flower lasts only a day. The China Rose is a dark bright red single flower. All varieties are scentless.

The fruit is a small hairy capsule which has five cells.

The flowers are used in cough syrups and hair oils. The bark of the shrub is made into a fibre.

30

EBONY

Latin Name	*Diospyros melanoxylon*
English Name	*Coromandel Ebony*
Indian Names	*Gujarati : Tamrug*
	Hindi : Tendu, Timburni
	Malayalam : Kari
	Marathi : Tumri
	Oriya : Kendu
	Sanskrit : Dirghapatraka
	Tamil : Karai, Tumbi
Family	Ebenaceae

Diospyros means Jove's Grain, referring to the edible fruit. The Sanskrit Dirghapatraka means long-leaved.

Why the tree has dark wood
(Tribal legend of the Konds of Ganjam)

When the Earth sank beneath the Great Flood, a Kond and his wife decided to seek shelter inside a gourd. They took a bundle of sticks with them so that they would have fire when they came out. They pulled the gourd shut after them and went to sleep.

Many many days later they awoke. They broke the gourd and saw that the water had dried and a new world awaited them. Thy emerged from the gourd carrying their bundle of sticks. The Kond lit a fire with the wood and the couple slept.

The next morning the Kond and his wife went to explore this new world. In their absence, a burnt twig

took root and grew into an ebony tree, and when they returned they saw it. The Tendu is black because it came from a charred piece of wood.

Black from venom
(A Kond legend)

Manglo Saora lived on the Mahendragiri mountain. He had five sons and three daughters. One day, when the family was cutting wood in the forest, the sons heard a loud shriek. The youngest daughter had been bitten by a poisonous snake and she lay dead on the ground, her face black. The family buried her at the same spot and from her grave grew the black Tendu tree.

It is a medium sized deciduous tree with a greyish-black bark. Its branches have spines on them.

The leaves grow alternately. They are egg-shaped to oblong, leathery and hairy underneath.

जुल्सिक